CCNA

Simple and Effective Strategies to Learn Routing and Switching Essentials

ETHAN THORPE

Table of Contents

Introduction

At present, the exchange of information is present in our daily lives, something that we need and with which we could not subsist. We can talk about the exchange of information at all levels, from basic communication based on a sender and a receiver to communication-based on a sender and multiple receivers. But what happens **when the exchange of information is between millions of senders and receivers?**

Nowadays, we cannot talk about information exchange without thinking about technologies, the Internet, or everything that surrounds us constantly, and the whole thing has a name: "telecommunication networks."

When we define the concept of a telecommunication network in the world of information technology, it is defined as: "A telecommunication network is a set of means (transmission and switching), technologies (processing, multiplexing, and modulation), protocols and facilities in general, necessary for the exchange of information among network users.

To be able to carry out these exchanges of information in the most optimal way, we must follow a series of procedures, regulations, and standards that are adequate to obtain the best performance.

In this book, we will cover the design, implementation, and administration of a local area network with external connections at the campus level, we will not focus on services, but on the design of the network, resources we need to implement it and its administration.

The network simulation will contain different parts of the university network design, for the implementation and administration of the network will be used interconnection devices such as:

- Routers Catalyst 2811.
- Fiber optic routers.
- WRT300N wireless Linksys routers.
- Catalyst S2000 switches.

For the implementation of the network, a series of protocols will be used justifying their use, the protocols that will be implemented are the following:

- RIPv2.
- OSPF.
- STP.
- VLAN's.
- VTP

- Trunks (802.1 Q protocol)
- EthernetChannel.
- FRAME RELAY
- Wireless.
- TFTP
- HTTP.
- NAT.
- PAT.

This book contains all the design, implementation and administration part of the network routing and switching, explaining how and why the network is designed in a certain way, how to implement it and how to manage the switching and routing analysis for the design of the network.

Topology

When designing a network, it is convenient to use the network topologies or physical structure of the network. Topologies describe the network physically and also provide us with information about the access method being used (Token Ring, Ethernet, etc.). Since the design is based on the university's network, we will use a star topology.

The star topology consists of several nodes connected to a central computer (in the example case, the central computer is the DPC under the central library). In a star design, the messages from each network node are passed directly to the central computer, which will determine where to route them, so it eventually becomes a mixed topology, star topology combined with ring topology. Some of the parts of the network will look like an extended star or tree topology.

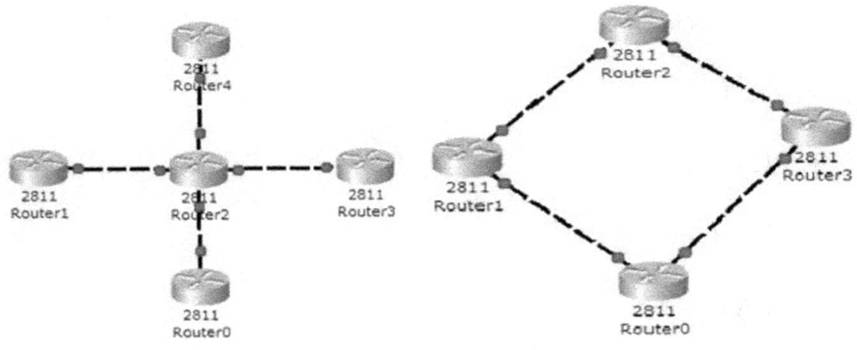

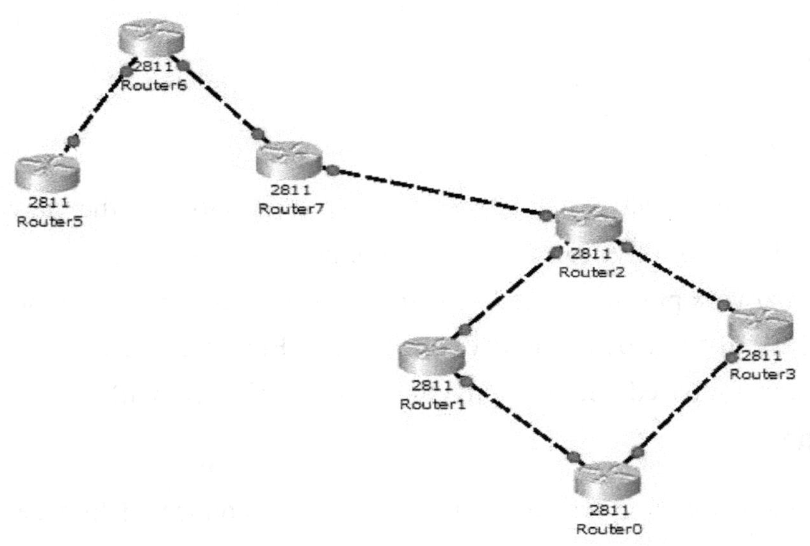

Due to the size of the university network, not all traffic will be routed to the core layer of the DPC, but part of the routing will be delegated to other routers around the campus.

Possible Problems of a Bad Network Design

Loss of Information

Information loss can be caused by many different factors, from network intrusion to poor design or implementation. Some of the factors for implementation are:

- **Network failures:** These network failures are mostly due to a bad connection to the Server, hubs, or a bad connection to the ISP.
- **Slow processing:** This may be due to not choosing the right hardware or not counting on the size of the network.

Protocols

TCP/IP:

The TCP/IP protocol is the most widespread in the world of telecommunications and is always referred to like one, but it is actually two protocols that work together to transmit data: the Transmission Control Protocol (TCP) and the Internet Protocol (IP).

The function of the TCP/IP protocol is to fragment the data into small packets when the packets arrive at their destination, and they are returned to their destination to de-fragment and return to their original form.

The TCP protocol splits the data into packets and regroups them when they reach their destination, while the IP protocol is responsible for handling the routing of the data and ensuring that it reaches the correct recipient.

Standard EIA/TIA 568

This is the standard created for the installation of Commercial Building Telecommunications, which can support a multi-product environment and multiple suppliers. In our case, although we are talking about the university network, we have some users to offer services, so we are talking about another company.

The purpose of this standard is to allow the design and installation of telecommunication cabling with little information about the systems that will be installed later. Installation of wiring systems during the installation and/or remodeling process is significantly cheaper and involves less disruption than after the building is completed.

The EIA/TIA 568A standard specifies the minimum requirements for commercial office cabling. Recommendations are made for:

- The topology
- The maximum distance of the cables
- The performance of the components
- Telecommunication sockets and connectors

The specified telecommunication cabling is intended to support various types of buildings and user applications. It is assumed that the buildings have the following characteristics:

- A distance between them of up to 3 km.
- Office space up to 1,000,000 m2
- A population of up to 50,000 individual users

Applications employing telecommunication cabling systems include, but are not limited to

- Voice, Data, Text, Video, Images

The service life of telecommunication cabling systems specified by this standard must be greater than ten years.

The benefits provided by the standard are: Flexibility, Ensures Technology Compatibility, Reduces Failures, Relocation, Additions, and Rapid Changes focusing on the design of the UPV.

Network Implementation

When implementing a network, several prerequisites must be taken into account to provide the network with everything it needs to function optimally. The right steps to take for good implementation:

Previous Knowledge

- Systems analysis and design.
- Legal (Laws, codes, regulations, agreements, ordinances, etc.)
- Technicians (current technologies and market availability)
- Network Services (communications service providers).

Description of the Network Request

- Problem Statement (why the network is being requested) Necessary information:
    - Tasks developed by the company.
    - Plans of the floor or floors and views of the buildings.
    - Identification of each sector.
    - Supply and distribution of electrical energy.
    - Telephone network.
    - Safety and protection systems (lightning rods, earthing, generator installations, if any, etc.).
    - Risks (floods, fires, etc.).

Investigation of the Applicant Company

Relief

- Prepare the forms for the disclosure.
- Details of existing equipment.
- Pre-existing facilities (not just previously installed computers).
- Statistical data
    - The number of transactions, local and remote.

- The number of telephone calls for operational reasons and administrative between the different sectors of the company.
- Use of email.
- Details of the sequence of operations (purchase orders, production, warehouse, shipping, etc.)

Network Definition

- Project
    - Selection of user equipment.
    - Selection of the necessary connectivity equipment.
    - Evaluation of the contracting of third party services.
    - Determination of alternatives.
    - Cost/benefit ratio.
    - Impact analysis and future growth.
        - Feasibility study.
        - Definitive design. Preparation of the final plans
        - Alternative projects.
        - Budgets.
        - Approval and/or acceptance of the applicant.

Network Installation

- Planning and scheduling of tasks. Coordination.
- Determination of installation times.
- Purchasing and contracting plans for media, equipment, and services. Installation.
    - Wired.
    - Connectivity equipment.
    - User equipment.
- Startup.
- Functional tests.
- Staff training Approval
- Delivery of the systems working.

Chapter One

Understand The Mpls Protocol: Concept, Technology, And Evolution

MPLS has become a technology that is the key to the future of IP networking. MPLS provides Traffic Engineering capabilities to packet-based networks, provides IP QoS capabilities, and helps build IP-based VPNs. These advances are critical to the success of multiservice providers.

MPLS is different from the hop-by-hop processing methods of traditional networks. A reduced fixed-size label provides a short form representation of the IP packet header just as the zip code is the short form for the street and city in a postal address.

Many proprietary commercial implementations of LBS are now available. CISCO with TAG switching; Ascend with IP Navigator; IBM with ARIS; Nokia with IP Switching. Each manufacturer has its own implementations of LBS, making it difficult to implement interoperable solutions.

Thus, as in other emerging standards, the ideas and experience of manufacturers and other researchers led to the implementation of a working group to study LBS-based solutions. This effort is being led by the Internet Engineering Task Force (IETF), seeking an open, interoperable, protocol-independent solution called Multiprotocol Label Switching (MPLS).

This chapter represents a study of technology and describes the reasons that led to its creation, what it does and the advantages that its use provides. MPLS standards promise to provide important interoperability functionality between different networking technologies; these are identified and discussed. The foundation of the "protocol" mechanism used in MPLS is introduced and its relationship to traditional routing mechanisms will be addressed.

Computer networks are gaining more and more space over the years. Not only the number of users grows, but also the variety of applications used. Therefore, the ideal is a multi-service platform that meets the needs of users in flexible bandwidth Internet Protocol (IP) -based services.

To meet this demand, Multiprotocol Label Switching (MPLS) has been developed to cover the majority of users and applications. It emerges as the leading technology that enables multiple network services over a shared infrastructure. This enables fast service provisioning by concentrating new and old.

MPLS can then be defined as a protocol developed for the transport of multimedia applications (voice, data, and video). It is a protocol technology based on improved traffic engineering methods since the 1990s, but only now has it been deployed on computer networks to create new services when both operators and equipment manufacturers have finally discovered their potential outside the scope of traffic engineering.

MPLS originated from connection-oriented networks, such as ATM networks, which, when launched, were intended to dominate the network market due to high speeds. However, Asynchronous Transfer Mode (ATM) technology was not compatible with IP, the most widespread network protocol in computer networks. For this reason, Label Based Switching (LBS) technology was created, enabling the best use of packet-based networks (IP networks) and connection-oriented networks (such as ATM networks).

What is MPLS?

The MPLS protocol is defined by the Internet Engineering Task Force (IETF) and consists of a packet switching technology that enables efficient routing and switching of traffic flows across the network, presenting itself as a solution to slow down equipment processing and connect networks of disparate technologies more effectively. The term Multiprotocol means that this technology can be used under any network protocol. Considering the Internet and the importance of its protocols in the various public and private wide area networks (WAN), the study and implementation of MPLS has been applied basically to IP networks.

MPLS provides Quality of Services (QoS), Traffic Engineering (VPN), and Virtual Private Network (VPN) services to an IP-based network. For applications that require real-time, QoS is implemented, which makes it possible to differentiate traffic types, giving priority to the most sensitive applications (scalable network).

How does MPLS work?

IP networks are widely used for business applications. However, they lack in the quality of service in circuit-based networks such as ATM, which companies are most used to. MPLS brings the sophistication of connection-oriented protocol to the connectionless IP world, thanks to simple advances in basic IP routing, providing better network performance and service creation capabilities.

When routing over a conventional IP network, an intense data search process is done based on the information contained in its headers and the information each router has about the range and availability of the other routers in the network. In MPLS networks, routers can decide the most appropriate routing based on labeled packets as they enter the network. This way, packets are forwarded only based on the contents of these labels, avoiding the whole conventional routing search process.

Forwarding packets considering the contents of their labels, rather than routing based on headers, has several significant advantages. For example, packet processing becomes faster since the time is taken to forward a label is less than the time taken to route a packet header. Priority can also be given to labels, which ensures Frame Relay and ATM quality of service. This process also allows packets to roam the public network through circuit-type static paths, which are the basis for VPNs. In addition, packet payload is not examined by forwarding routers, allowing for different levels of encryption and the transport of multiple protocols.

To provide IP-based services, MPLS is used by the carrier to map the customer's private IP network to the public network and to assemble virtual routing tables for the network, routing data, and route information to other sites than the customer. It has. By changing the IP topology of the client network, this change is immediately communicated to other client sites through the public network.

Operators can use MPLS to establish virtual circuits or tunnels on an IP network. Another use is that operators with IP, Frame Relay, and ATM networks can use MPLS to interconnect them, avoiding high hardware upgrades for both customers and providers.

In summary, MPLS aims to be a method that manages a certain switching structure under any datagram network, using routes organized by network layer routing protocols to create virtual circuits. The process consists of processing and dividing the information into classes of service (assigning labels) and routing the data through routes previously established by these classes, only switching. The link level is preserved, and MPLS can be applied to Ethernet, ATM, and Frame Relay networks, for example.

Speed, scalability, quality of service management (QoS), and the need for traffic engineering are problems that computer networks currently face. MPLS is a technology used in backbones and aims to solve these problems. For this reason, it is now recognized as the leading technology capable of delivering differentiated services that meet the diverse needs of network users, from small businesses using the network to negotiate with their customers and suppliers, to large ones that are implementing a global VPN.

The Beginning of MPLS

The TCP / IP protocol (especially the IP protocol itself) is the foundation for today's public networks (the Internet, for example) and private data networks (corporate intranet). With the advent of convergence of voice, data, and multimedia networks, it is expected that most of the IP protocols will be used, creating a need for technical and operational improvements in this protocol. Switching using tags is one of the industry's answers to this challenge.

Improving the original architecture of TCP / IP has been a major goal in recent times. For example, IP networks need to evolve to support real-time packet delivery, IP integration with ATM protocols, creation of virtual public networks, and the creation of much larger public networks. Improving efficiency with increased performance and lower costs (which may encourage VoIP use, for example) would lead to radical changes in telecommunications. Using label switching for QoS support and providing attributes for traffic engineering are seen as part of the solution.

Label switching solutions can be characterized by tagged packet routing combined with IP control protocols and tag distribution mechanisms.

One of the biggest problems for network engineers is solving the integration problems between IP and ATM. The difficulties encountered with the mapping between IP protocol and ATM served as a driver for the development of label switching technology. Over the past five years, several companies have invested in the development of technologies that combine ATM's high-speed operation with IP-based network layer processes. The following are four of these companies:

a) The Cell Switching Router (CSR) - developed by Toshiba and introduced to the IETF in 1994. It is designed to function as a router to logically connect subnets in a classic "IP over ATM" environment. Tag switching devices communicate over standard ATM virtual circuits. Tagging by CSRs is data-driven (i.e., tags are assigned on the basis of streams that are locally identified). The Flow Attribute Notification Protocol (FANP) is used to identify virtual circuits (VCs) between CSRs and establish the association between individual flows and virtual circuits. CSRs have been developed in Japan's business and academic networks.

b) IP Switching, developed by Ipsilon (now part of Nokia), was announced in early 1996 and was used in commercial products. IP Switching allows an ATM switch to act as a router, thereby exceeding the packet throughput limit of traditional routers. The basic purpose of IP Switching is to integrate ATM switches and IP routers simply and efficiently (eliminating the ATM control plan). IP Switching uses the presence of data traffic to lead to the establishment of a tag. A flow management protocol (Ipsilon Flow Management Protocol or IFMP) and a switch management protocol

(GSMP) are defined. GSMP is used solely to control an ATM switch and the virtual circuits produced by it.

c) Tag Switching is the tag switching technology developed by CISCO. In contrast to previous techniques, Tag Switching is a control-oriented technique that does not rely on data flow to encourage tagging on router routing tables. A Tag Switching network consists of label collation edge routers and label switching routers. Standard IP routing protocols are used to determine the next hop. Tags are coupled to routers in routing tables and distributed to neighbors via Tag Distribution Protocol.

d) Aggregate Route-based IP Switching (ARIS) was developed by IBM and is similar to the Tag Switching architecture.

Change in Current Networks

The network engineer today faces the demands that only dreamed when IP was first set in 1970. Today's networks need to support ever-increasing volumes of data on the Internet traditionally (using file transfer, e-mail, and www.) and differentiation is also being required between the various traffic classes, which may include voice, music, and video.

Quality of service has turned into a cheering cry for those who see a global IP convergence across all forms of communication. The potentials of the underlying elements of the network - the routers and switches that run the protocols - have become critical to this process. However, many experts believe that traditional hop-by-hop processing is reaching its technological limit and that a change in the current paradigm is necessary for the evolutionary process of network technologies. The challenge is to evolve the IP network architecture, preparing it for the arrival of the next generation of networks, enabling a smooth and cost-effective transition.

One factor must be considered - the production of faster and cheaper routers. The explosive growth of the Internet and the projected expansion of many millions of IP addresses have placed it in the spotlight (and router manufacturers have responded with higher capacity routers). The development of label switching technology, however, is being driven not only by the need for higher speed. Two significant aspects are:

- Different classes of traffic require specific service characteristics that must be ensured throughout the network (and often across multiple autonomous systems);

- IP multi-user infrastructure requires robust networks that require more efficient resource management.

The efficient use of network resources is one of the biggest goals for new network technology. MPLS traffic engineering capabilities allow a degree of control over network behavior that conventional IP technologies do not have.

Today's networks face key challenges in the following areas:

a) Functionality - Label switching provides new functions that were inefficient or unavailable in conventional routing.

Explicit routing selects a specific route that need not be the shortest route, for example. Choosing a route taking into account the attributes can be, for example, choosing a route based on the required QoS.

b) Scalability - Future networks need to be virtually unlimited in size. Routing information grows very rapidly as the network grows, and can eventually overload a router. Traffic Engineering, in this case, allows for greater efficiency in the use of network resources helping in its scalability.

c) Possibility of Evolution - One of the biggest challenges will be to allow change and growth without interrupting the network. Deterministic services need to be covered in a non-deterministic network like IP, multiple IP traffic needs to be accepted, and virtual private networks need to be created and removed.

d) Integration - Converging applications for IP phones is an example of system integration.

Several basic concepts that apply to switching technology need to be reviewed before describing how MPLS works.

a) Routing is a term used to describe actions taken by the network to move packets through it. We speak packets that are routed from A to B or are being routed on a network or an internal network. Packets travel across the network and are sent from machine to machine until they reach their destination. The routing protocol (e.g., RIP, OSPF) enables each machine to understand which other machine is the next-hop a packet must make to reach its destination. Routers use routing protocols to build routing tables. When they receive a packet and have to make a forwarding decision, routers look up the routing table using the IP address of the destination in the packet, thereby obtaining the identity of the next hop machine. Logical operations can separate the construction of tables and their use for forwarding.

b) Switching is generally used to describe the transfer of data from an input port to an output port where the choice of the output port is based on layer two information (e.g., ATM VPI / VCI).

c) The control component builds and maintains the routing table of the node in use. It works with control components from other nodes to distribute routing information consistently and accurately, and also ensures local procedures that are used in routing tables. Standard routing protocols (for example, OSPF, BGP, and RIP) are used to exchange routing information between control components. The control component needs to react when network changes occur (such as link failure) but are not involved in individual packet processing.

d) Routing components perform packet forwarding. They use the information from the routing table (which is maintained by the router); This information is loaded into the package itself, and a set of local procedures make the routing decision. In conventional routing, an algorithm compares the destination address in the packet with an entry in the routing table until an advantageous value is found. This entire process is repeated on each node from the source from source to destination. In LSR, tag swapping algorithms use packet tags and the tag-based routing table to get a new tag and output interface for the packet.

e) The routing table is a set of entries in a table that provides information that helps routing components perform switching functions. The forwarding table needs to associate each packet with an entry (traditionally the destination address) to provide instructions on where the packet should go. LFIB - Table indicating where and how to forward packets. Created by equipment belonging to an MPLS domain, the LFIB contains a list of entries that consist of an ingress sub-entry and one or more egress sub-entries (exit label, exit interface, link-level exit components).). LFIB is constructed based on information obtained by LSR through interaction with routing protocols.

f) Forwarding Equivalence Class (FEC) is defined as a group of packets that can be treated equivalently. An example of an FEC would be a set of unicast packets whose destination addresses match a specific IP address prefix. Another FEC is the set of packets whose source and destination addresses are the same.

g) A label is a relatively short identifier and a fixed length that is used in the packet forwarding process. Tags are associated with an FEC in a required MPLS process. Tags are usually local to a data link and have no global meaning (such as an address). Labels are analogous to DLCI used in a Frame Relay network or VPI / VCIs used in an ATM environment. ATM is a technology that already uses short length fixed fields to make routing decisions. Tags are restricted by the FEC, resulting from some events that indicate the needs in the link.

Label Switching

There are three important differences between label switching and conventional routing:

A *Label Switching Router* is a device that supports both IP control components (i.e., routing protocols, RSVP, etc.) and label routing and exchange components. The following figure simply exemplifies a label switching network and illustrates Edge LSRs (provides network input and output functions) and Core LSRs (performs high-speed switching). A label switching network has the same purpose as traditional routing networks: to deliver traffic to one or more destinations.

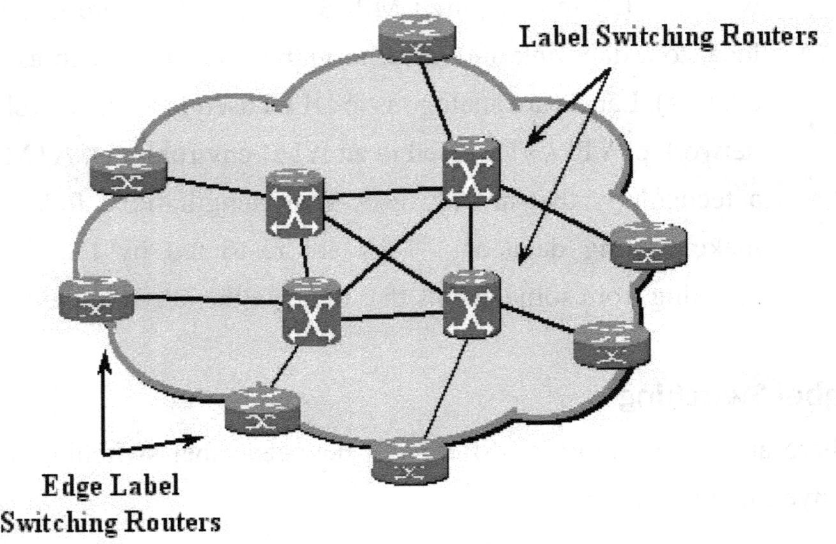

Routing Components

A tag can be associated with a package in several ways. Some networks may label the data-link layer header (on ATM VCI / VPI, and Frame Relay DLCI). Another option is to place it between the Layer 2 and Layer 3 header. These techniques allow tag switching to support any type of data link, including Ethernet, FDDI, and peer-to-peer links.

At the boundary of an MPLS network, edge routers classify packets by examining their IP header. Appropriate labels are applied to the packets and then forwarded by the LSR.

"Labels" act as a header representation of IP packets, and through their use, processing complexity is reduced over subsequent nodes. The tag is generated during LSR node header processing. All subsequent nodes in the network use the tag for their forwarding decisions. Label values need, and do, change with each LSR. This is done until the packet reaches the edge LSR at the network exit.

When a packet enters an LSR, it parses its label and uses it as an index to search its routing table. From this index (input tag), an entry (or more) is searched in the routing table. If the entry is found, the tag is replaced with the exit tag pointed to in the routing table entry, and the exit interface sends the packet to the next hop.

What is most important about tag-based routing is that only a single routing algorithm is needed for the entire switching model.

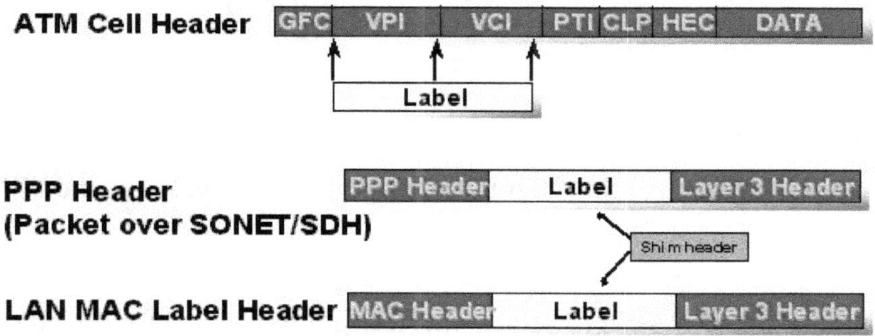

Label Placement in Different Headers

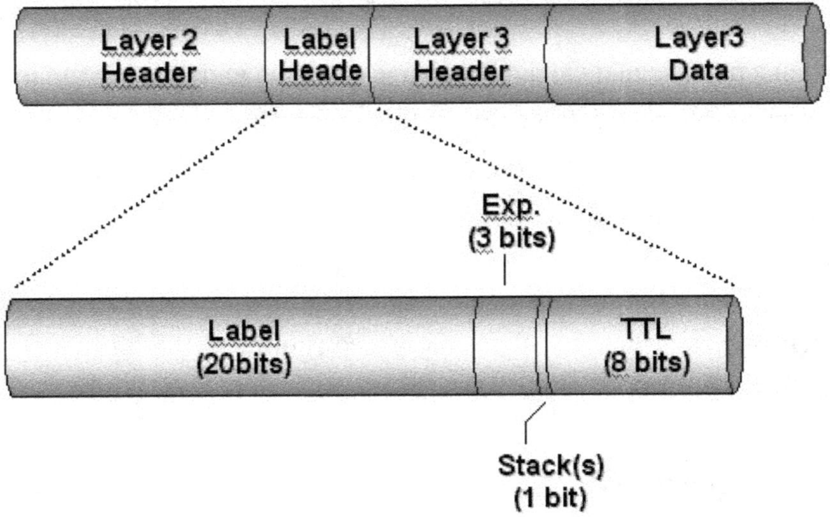

MPLS Label

1. The *Label* field (20 bits) carries the current value of the MPLS label;

2. The *EXP* field (3 bits) Experimental bits. Used for the class of service, they can affect the queuing and discarding algorithms applied to the packet as it is transmitted over the network;

3. The *Stack* field (1 bit) supports a hierarchical stack of labels;

4. The *TTL* field (8 bits) provides conventional IP TTL functionality.

Control Components

The labels are placed by the LSR, who will send the package. The LSR that receives this tagged packet needs to know what to do with it. It is the responsibility of the control component to take on this task. It uses the routing table input content as a guide.

Establishing and maintaining the routing table entry are essential functions performed by each LSR. The tracking component is responsible for distributing distribution information consistently among LSRs and performing the procedures that are used by LSRs to convert this information to a forwarding table.

Label switching control components include all conventional distribution protocols (e.g., OSPF, BGP, PIM, and so on). These distribution protocols provide LSRs with information on how to map between the FEC and next-hop equipment addresses. In addition, the LSR must:

- Create the link between the tags and the FECs;
- Distribute these links to other LSRs;
- Build your own forwarding table.

The link between a tag and an FEC can be data-driven (i.e., is the result of the presence of specific types of traffic flow) or can control is driven (i.e., whether driven by routing update topology or other control messages).

Each of these linking techniques has numerous options. The decision to establish the flow can be based on several criteria. Tag binding, in the data-driven case, establishes active tags only when there is an immediate need (i.e., when traffic is presented for routing). Topology change or traffic change information needs to be distributed. In the control-oriented case, the connection is based on the knowledge resulting from the routing and reservation procedure.

Tag Distribution Information

Inputting a routing table provides, at a minimum, information about the output interface and the new label, but also contains other information. It can, for example, indicate the method of queuing on the output to be applied to the package.

Each tag that is distributed must be limited to one entry in the routing table. This connection can be performed on the local LSR or provided by a remote LSR.

The MPLS architecture uses local control (LSR can create and announce a call without waiting for neighbor communication over the same FEC) and output control (LSR expects communication from its neighbor before allocating a tag).

The knowledge between locally chosen links and associated FECs should be disseminated to adjacent LSRs for this information to be used in constructing routing tables. The information in the routing table should also follow changes in the network. After all, the label on the incoming packet is used to find out the rules for packet forwarding.

Tag information can be distributed in two ways:

a) Adding in Routing Protocols

Information can be added to traditional routing protocols, although only control-oriented schemas can support this method. Switching to normal protocol operations ensures consistency in routing information and avoids the need for other protocols.

b) Use of the Label Distribution Protocol

Following the CISCO Tag Switching model, the MPLS definition group has created a new specific label distribution protocol called the Label Distribution Protocol (LDP). LDP can be used in both data-driven and control-oriented schemas. The disadvantage of LDP is that it adds complexity.

Label Stack

The tag stack mechanism allows you to perform a hierarchical operation on the MPLS domain by including more than one tag in a packet. This stacking allows network core LSRs to exchange information with each other and act as edge routers. These new "edge" routers define a new MPLS domain. Within a large network, we may have multiple domains. For each, we will have an associated tag level. This technique allows you to shrink the routing tables of the MPLS network inbound routers.

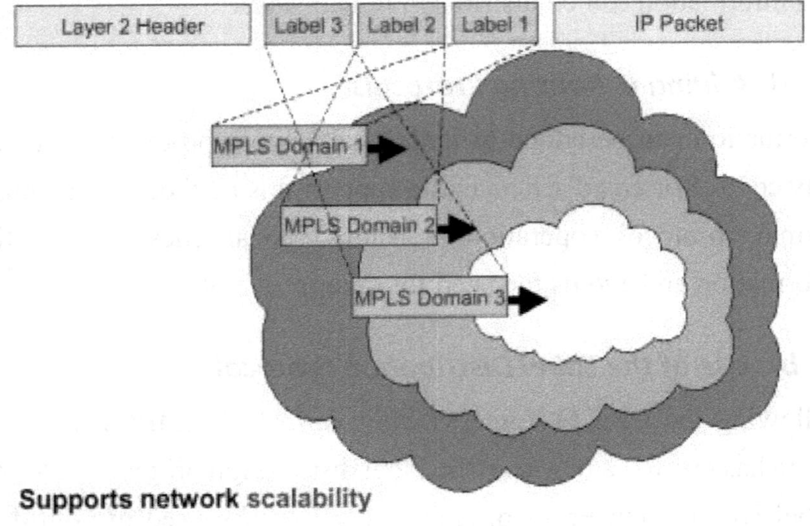

The Role of Edge Routers (ELSR)

It is the responsibility of Edge Label Switching Routers (ELSRs) to classify traffic and apply (remove) labels from packets. As has been seen earlier, tags can be assigned based on QoS requirements rather than their destination address as traditional routing does. ELSR determines if traffic is a steady stream and implements management and access control policies.

Thus, the ability of ELSRs is the key to the success of a label switching environment. It is also a point of control and management of service providers.

New generations of ELSR need to have the following capabilities:

- IP stream rating capability: This will allow these devices to assign QoS values and apply tags to the IP without any degradation in routing performance;

- Extensive VPN Capability: These devices need to run multiple routing tables so that VPN clients can separate their traffic.

Label Switching Path (LSP)

An MPLS device set represents an MPLS domain. Within an MPLS domain, a path is created for a given packet based on its FEC. This path is formed by an ordered sequence of LSRs, established between a source and a destination within the same domain. This formed path is known as the Label Switched Path (LSP).

The LSP is adjusted before data transmission. It is done with conventional routing protocols or restricted routing. It is important to note that an LSP is unidirectional, so you must have two LSPs for communication between two entities.

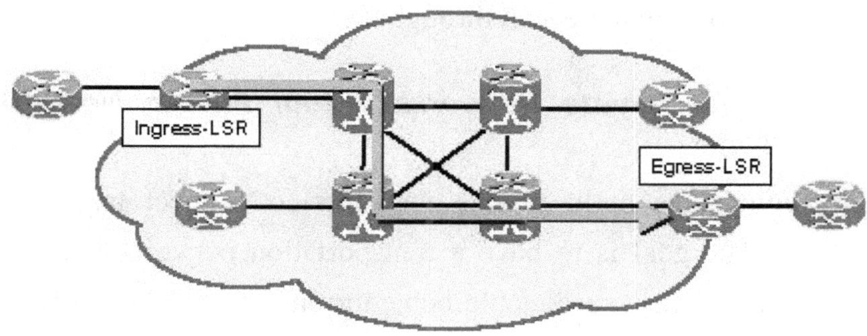

MPLS Advantages

The main benefit of MPLS is that it is the basis of the standard for the technology based on label switching. Developing standard outcomes in the open-source environment with various manufacturers producing interoperable equipment. The competition is also resulting the prices to lower and leads to greater innovation.

The question is: *What are the benefits and advantages of using label switching? Is tag switching a necessary step in the evolution of TCP / IP architecture?*

a) Explicit Routing

Explicit routing is a powerful technique that can be applied for a variety of purposes. For many applications, implicit routing based on packet-to-packet datagram analysis generates an often unacceptable overhead. MPLS allows packets to be classified from tags assigned upon admission of MPLS nodes and routed within the same class on a virtual path without the need to be parsed node by node. Explicit routing also has the advantage of creating "transparent tunnels" through which any traffic (e.g., SNA, IPX) travels. LSRs "see" only the packet labels that are sent through the tunnel.

b) Virtual Private Networks (Virtual Private Networks, VPN)

Many companies build private networks to connect to multiple locations. The goal is to have a transportation network that offers security, reliability, predictable behavior and is cheaper. VPNs are generally an imitation of this private network. MPLS is the key element in constructing these networks; we can use the MPLS tags to separate the traffic between VPNs.

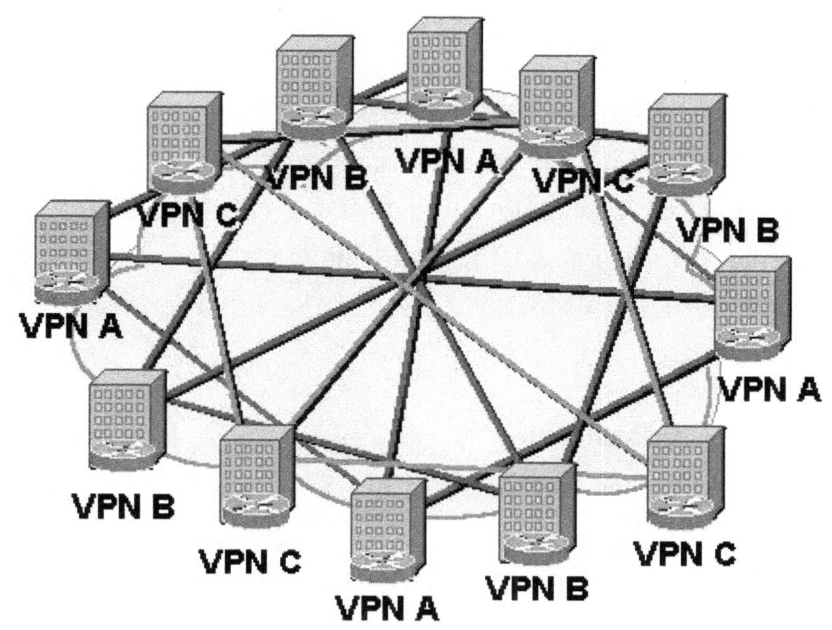

Traditional VPN

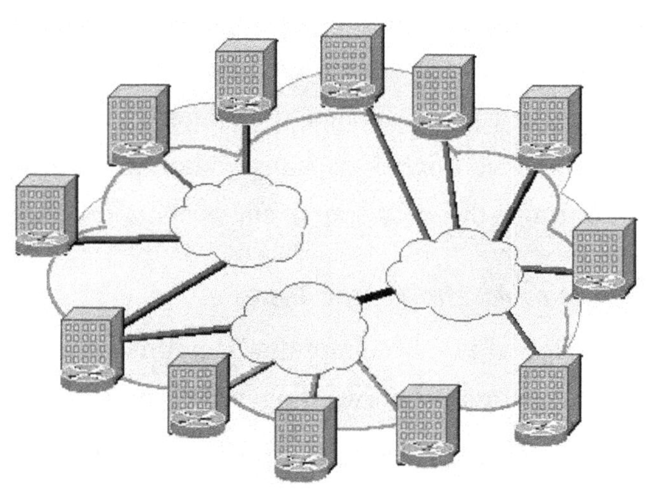

c) Multiple Protocol and Multiple Link Support

The routing element is not precise to a network layer. It is possible to use the same routing component to do IP tag switching, and IPX tag switching, for example. Label switching can operate over the protocols of the data link layer, even if the initial importance was focused on the ATM.

d) Ease of Evolution

Label switching has the benefit of providing a separation between control and routing functions. Every single part can function flawlessly without creating an impact on any other part, and this makes network evolution easier, cost-effective, and less error-prone.

e) Interdomain Routing

Tag switching provides complete separation between intra-domain and inter-domain distribution. This improves scalability in the routing process and cuts the required knowledge of a route within a domain. Generally, it is an advantage to Internet Service Providers (ISPs) and bearers who might have a high amount of traffic in transit (that is, traffic from a different source and destination networks).

f) Support to All the Traffic Types

Another advantage of tag switching that is not usually visible to the user is that it supports all forwarding types: unicast, service-type unicast, and multicast packets. It can be used with attribution of QoS, which consecutively permits diverse classes of ISP access services to be defined.

MPLS provides a significant improvement in the packet forwarding process due to its simplicity, avoiding the need to perform IP header parsing along the way, and creating a controlled QoS support environment. Several manufacturers have developed different label switching techniques, and MPLS has emerged as a standard that has unified these technologies. MPLS enables the integration of IP with ATM and many other layers, layer 2, and layer three technologies; supports the convergence of services (voice, data, and video); offers new opportunities to Traffic Engineering and VPN support.

Adding reduced fixed-size labels, just as CEP helps in sorting cards, packet processing performance is improved, and QoS control can be easily applied.

MPLS is a flexible technology that allows it to be mapped across various network technologies. Its feature of interconnecting IP routers makes it a reference for building networks that provide convergence of telephone, video, and computer services.

Chapter Two

VLAN features and configuration

This chapter presents the basic characteristics of VLANs (Virtual Local Area Network), their advantages, and basic switch configuration. An explanation of its fundamentals is given, as well as its implementation step by step, through various means, so that its operation can be understood and its basic configuration learned, laying the foundations for progress in the implementation and management of VLANs.

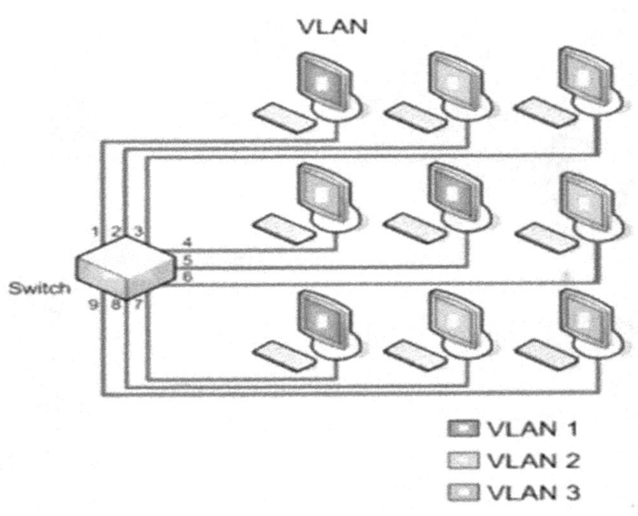

VLANs, Acronym Virtual Local Area Network (the network of the virtual local area) is one or more logical networks that coexist within a single physical network, and what would be its usefulness? The best known is to divide a single broadcast domain into several smaller broadcast domains, also for a security issue to have separate networks that are a priority of user networks.

A Virtual Local Area Network (VLAN) is a flexible group of devices that are located anywhere on a local area network but communicate as if they were on the same physical segment. With VLANs, the network can be segmented without being restricted to physical locations or connections.

The advantages that VLANs can bring us are among others:

- Greater flexibility and better resource management by facilitating the change and movement of devices on the network.
- Easy troubleshooting and isolation.
- Improved security due to separation of devices into different VLANs
- *Broadcast* traffic control.
- Separation of protocols.

They can be implemented according to various criteria such as the ports of a switch to which the computers are connected, MAC addresses, etc. In this chapter, we will present the first option.

After reading this chapter carefully, you will be able to

- Take advantage of the features and benefits provided by VLANs
- Identify details of implementation and operation of VLANs
- Set up basic VLANs.

Each of the aspects indicated in the introduction and objectives will then be developed, making the explanations as practical and guided as possible.

The History of VLANs

When the 1980s had just begun, Ethernet was already a technology that was consolidated and offered speeds of up to 1 Mbps / s, which was much higher than the vast majority of alternatives that existed at that time.

At this time, the big problem that had to be solved in Ethernet networks is that they had a bus topology used as a physical means of transmission the coaxial cable, which was shared. Therefore, Ethernet was a broadcast network, and as such, when two stations transmit simultaneously, collisions occur and bandwidth is wasted on failed transmissions.

So we can conclude that at this time the Ethernet did not offer scalability, since, when the network increased greatly in size, its benefits decrease.

The Carrier sense multiple access with collision detection, better known as CSMA / CD, imposes limitations on the maximum bandwidth and maximum distance between two stations. Connecting multiple Ethernet networks was complicated at that time since the routers for interconnection were expensive and required a longer processing time per large packet, which ended up increasing the delay.

Thinking of a way to solve these problems, W. Kempf invented a device that worked in layer 2 of Model OSI, using software to interconnect two LANs, this device is known as Bridge or Bridge.

In 1989 a company called Kalpana developed the first seven-port Ethernet switch, multi-port bridge implemented in hardware, level 2 frame switching device.

The use of switches to interconnect Ethernet networks allows the collision domains to be separated, which greatly increases the efficiency and scalability of the Ethernet network.

This new network that is now growing in size needs to be fault-tolerant and have a high level of availability, and that requires that redundant topologies be used: multiple links between switches and redundant equipment. In this way, in the event of a single point failure, it is possible to recover the service automatically and quickly.

This new design of redundant Ethernet networks requires the enablement of a new protocol, the spanning tree or simply STP, comes to ensure that there is only one logical path to go from one node to another, thus avoiding the phenomenon known as broadcast storms.

Everything was going well, but, in this logical network topology, the core switches become bottlenecks, since most of the network traffic circulates through them.

It was there that finally, David Sincoskie managed to alleviate the overhead of the switches by creating the virtual LANs, by adding a tag to the Ethernet frames with which it was possible to differentiate the traffic.

At the moment we define several different VLANs, each of them will have its own spanning tree, and you can assign the different ports of a switch to each of these VLANs. For these VLANs to be able to walk between the various switches in the Ethernet network, without having to have a link between switches for each of the existing VLANs, a special link was created that we call a trunk.

Today the use of VLANs is widespread in modern Ethernet networks, yet, using them for the original purpose is usually somewhat strange since it is usual to use them to separate broadcast domains (hosts that can be reached by a frame broadcast)

VLAN Rating

Level 1 VLAN (per port). Also known as "port switching." It specifies which ports of the switch belong to the VLAN, the members of that VLAN are those that connect to those ports.

Level 2 VLAN by MAC addresses. Hosts are assigned to a VLAN based on their MAC address. It has the advantage that the switching device does not have to be reconfigured if the user changes its location; that is, it is connected to another port of that or another device. The main drawback is that if there are hundreds of users, the members should be assigned one by one.

Level 2 VLAN by protocol type. The VLAN is determined by the content of the protocol type field of the MAC frame. For example, VLAN 1 would be associated with the IPv4 protocol, VLAN 2 with the IPv6 protocol, VLAN 3 with AppleTalk, VLAN 4 with IPX, and others

Level 3 VLAN by subnet addresses. The level 3 header is used to map the VLAN to which it belongs. In this type of VLAN, it is the packets and not the stations that belong to the VLAN. Stations with multiple network protocols (level 3) will be on multiple VLANs.

VLAN of higher levels. A VLAN is created for each application: FTP, multimedia streams, email, among others. Membership of a VLAN can be based on a combination of factors such as ports, MAC addresses, subnet, time of day, method of access, equipment security conditions, among others.

Static VLAN or Dynamic VLAN

- ***Static:*** Static (or port-based) VLANs are created when they are attributed to each port of a switch to a VLAN. When a new device connects to the network, it assumes the VLAN of the port to which it is connected. In case of change, if that device is going to be connected to a new port, for example, so that it remains in the same original VLAN, it will be necessary for the network administrator to reconfigure the new port on the same VLAN manually.

- ***Dynamic:*** Dynamic VLANs are created and dynamically changed by software through a VMPS server (VLAN Management Policy Server), which is a database that stores the data of all VLAN participants. Dynamic VLANs are based on the criteria set by the network administrator, such as the MAC address or the name of the network usage of each device connected to the switch.

VLAN Related Protocols

When it is necessary to configure one or more VLANs, the participation of a series of protocols is necessary, among which IEEE 802.1Q, STP, and VTP (Cisco Owner) or GVRP (Defined by IEEE) stand out.

IEEE 802.1Q

The moment you start hearing a little more about VLANs, you will see that the IEEE 802.1Q protocol is the great star since it is responsible for the labeling of the frames that are immediately associated with the VLAN information.

Still, just as today the IEEE 802.1Q tagging protocol is the most common star for VLAN tagging, before its introduction, there were several proprietary protocols, such as the Cisco Inter-Switch Link

(ISL), a variant of the IEEE 802.1Q, and the VLT (Virtual LAN Trunk) of 3Com.

The IEEE 802.1Q is characterized by using a frame format similar to 802.3 (Ethernet) where only the value of the Ethertype field changes, which in the 802.1Q frames is worth 0x8100, and two bytes are added to encode the priority, the CFI and the VLAN ID This protocol is an international standard and compatible with bridges and switches without VLAN capability.

It's a modification to the Ethernet standard. The IEEE 802.1Q protocol was a project of the IEEE 802 Working Group to develop a mechanism to allow multiple bridged or switched networks to transparently share the same physical medium without interference problems between the networks sharing the medium (trunking). It is also the current name of the standard established in this project and is used to define the encapsulation protocol used to implement this mechanism in Ethernet networks.

It allows identifying a frame as coming from a computer connected to a certain network. A frame belonging to a VLAN will only be distributed to computers belonging to the same VLAN, so broadcast domains are separated.

Frame Format

The 802.1Q protocol proposes adding 4 bytes to the original Ethernet header instead of encapsulating the original frame. The value of the EtherType field is changed to 0x8100 to indicate the change in the frame format.

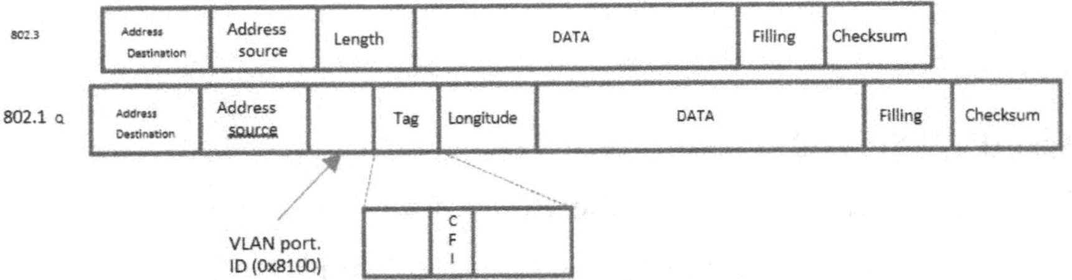

As shown in the above figure, the VLAN tag is inserted into the Ethernet frame between the "Source address" and "Length" fields. The first 2 bytes of the VLAN tag consists of the 802.1Q "Tag Type" and is always set to 0x8100. The last 2 bytes contain the following information:

- The first 3 bits are the User Priority Field, which is used to assign a priority level.
- The next bit is the Canonical Format Indicator (CFI) field used to indicate a Routing Information Field (RIF).
- The remaining 12 bits are the VLAN Identifiers (VID) that uniquely identify the VLAN to which the Ethernet frame belongs to.

Spanning Tree Protocol (STP)

The main task of Spanning Tree Protocol (STP) is to prevent the appearance of logical loops so that there is only one path between two nodes. Thus we can avoid the saturation of the switches due to broadcast storms, a network with redundant topology, as already said before, the STP protocol must be enabled.

The switches that have Spanning Tree Protocol enabled exchange STP BPDU (Bridge Protocol Data Units) messages with each other so that the network topology is a tree and only one path has been activated to go from one node to another.

Rapid Spanning Tree Protocol (RSTP) specified in IEEE 802.1w, is an evolution of the Spanning tree Protocol (STP), which significantly reduces the convergence time of the network topology when a change in the topology occurs.

MSTP (IEEE 802.1Q) allows you to create different expansion trees and assign them to different VLAN groups through configuration. This allows you to use links in a tree that are locked in another tree.

VLAN Trunking Protocol (VTP)

The VTP uses level 2 frames to manage the creation, deletion, and renaming of VLANs in a network, synchronizing all devices. For that, you must first establish a VTP management domain, which is a contiguous set of switches linked with trunk links that have the same VTP domain name.

There are three different ways in which the switches can be configured:

1. ***Server:*** This mode is the one that is configured by default on the switches, it announces its configuration to the rest of the equipment and synchronizes with other VTP servers.

2. ***Client:*** In this mode, the switches cannot modify the configuration of the VLANs; it simply synchronizes the configuration based on the information sent by the servers.

3. ***Transparent:*** When a switch is in transparent mode, the configuration of the VLANs must be done manually since this equipment will ignore all the messages sent by the VTP.

One of the functions of the VTP is pruning (pruning), which tries to keep on a path, only VLANs that have a port configured on the switches that are later in this path.

Port Types on Switches

There are two types of ports:

1. Access Ports

The stations are connected directly. They map the port to a programmed VLAN. When an Ethernet frame enters, the 802.1Q TAG is added. When an 802.1Q frame is an output, the TAG is removed, so that it arrives at the corresponding station with the original IEEE 802.3 format.

2. Ports 1Q Trunk

They are used to connect switches to each other and let traffic from different VLANs pass through them. The incoming and outgoing frames carry the 802.1Q tag.

Native VLANs

The standard defines the encapsulation protocol used to multiplex multiple VLANs over a single link and introduces the concept of native VLANs. Frames belonging to native VLANs are not changed when sent via trunking. Native VLANs are also known as "management VLANs" since the computers connected to these VLANs will be the ones from which we will configure the switches and will be able to manage the VLANs.

Manufacturers generally ship their equipment with the id 1 VLAN configured as a native VLAN, default VLAN, and management VLAN. This means that by default, all ports on the switch belong to VLAN 1. If a port is added to another VLAN created later, it will no longer belong to the management VLAN. You can only have one native VLAN per port.

VLAN Configuration Via TELNET Access to the Switch

First of all, make sure that the computer used to set up the VLANs in the switch is connected to the switch via the corresponding network cable. Then we'll type in: telnet <dir. Switch IP>. When accessing via Telnet, the first thing that appears is a menu with several options, as we can see in the below figure.

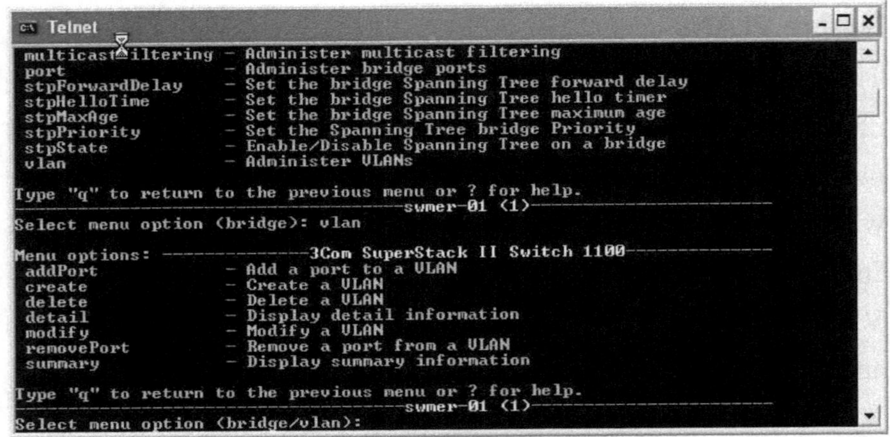

Telnet
multicastFiltering - Administer multicast filtering
port - Administer bridge ports
stpForwardDelay - Set the bridge Spanning Tree forward delay
stpHelloTime - Set the bridge Spanning Tree hello timer
stpMaxAge - Set the bridge Spanning Tree maximum age
stpPriority - Set the Spanning Tree bridge Priority
stpState - Enable/Disable Spanning Tree on a bridge
vlan - Administer VLANs
Type "q" to return to the previous menu or ? for help.
swmer-01 (1)
Select menu option (bridge): vlan
Menu options: 3Com SuperStack II Switch 1100
addPort - Add a port to a VLAN
create - Create a VLAN
delete - Delete a VLAN
detail - Display detail information
modify - Modify a VLAN
removePort - Remove a port from a VLAN
summary - Display summary information
Type "q" to return to the previous menu or ? for help.
swmer-01 (1)
Select menu option (bridge/vlan):

With the "bridge" option, we manage the VLANs.

Type "VLAN" to access the options for VLAN management: create, delete, modify a VLAN, add and remove ports of a VLAN and display information.

Creating VLANs on a Switch

A VLAN is defined by:

- A VLAN name: descriptive name for the VLAN (sales, accounting, etc.)
- A VLAN ID: the identifier of the VLAN created.
- A Local ID: identifies the VLAN locally in the stack.

For example, we can create a VLAN with ID 400:

Enter VLAN ID (2-4094)	:	400
Enter LocalID (2-16)	:	4

Enter VLANName [VLAN 200]: VLAN 400

Adding Ports to a VLAN

The ports where the workstations are connected, should not be configured as tagged, we will only configure in such a way the ports that we use to connect switches to each other.

Type in the "addPort" option

Select VLAN ID (1-4094) [1]: 400

Select Ethernet port (1-14,all): 5

Enter tag type (none, 802.1Q) [802.1Q]: none

Get Details of a VLAN

With the option "detail," we select the VLAN on which we want to obtain information, and we see its VLAN ID, the Local ID, the Name and the ports it contains.

With the option "summary" all the above is displayed, except the ports.

Changing a VLAN port

To do this, we will first use the "removePort" option and then "addPort."

Configure the Ports that Connect Switches as 802.1x Ports (Tagged Ports)

The format of the command to be used will be: bridge VLAN addport vlan_created 802.1Q tag port

Where Port tag is the port that connects the 2 Switches with a crossover cable. Here is an example:

bridge VLAN addport 400 16 802.1q

bridge VLAN addport 500 16 802.1q

Configuration of VLANs via HTTP

It is also possible to create and configure VLANs by accessing the corresponding switch via HTTP using a web browser. An example of this is shown in Figure 3. To do this, you must connect to the switch by entering a URL of the type: http://<dir. IP of the switch>, and once the initial page has been loaded, browse through the different options.

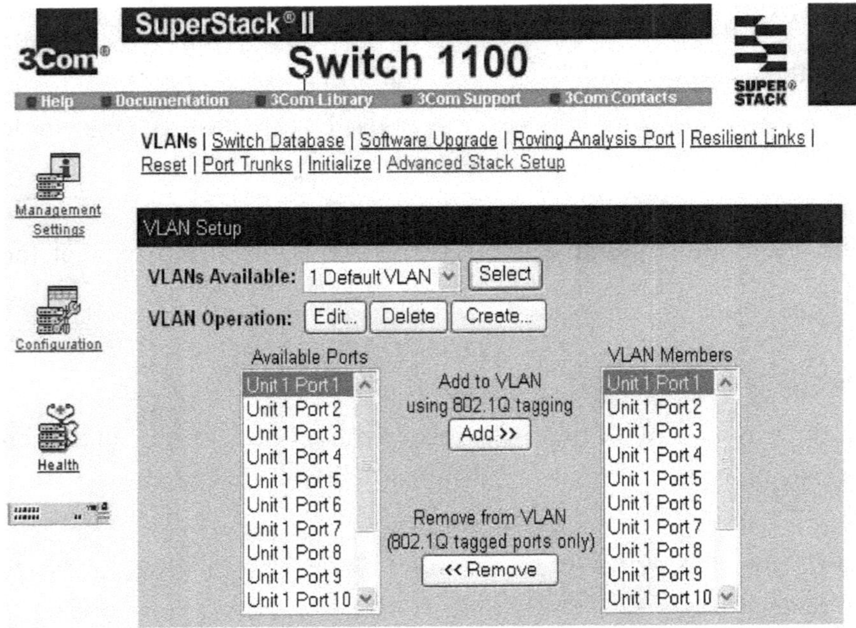

VLAN Design

Early network designers used to configure VLANs to reduce the size of the collision domain in an Ethernet segment and thus improve its performance.

When the switches achieved this, because each port is a collision domain, their priority was to reduce the size of the broadcast domain. Since, if the number of terminals increases, diffusion traffic and CPU consumption increase due to the processing of unwanted broadcast traffic.

One of the most efficient ways to reduce the broadcast domain is with the division of a large network into several VLANs.

The Design of Current Corporate Networks

Modern corporate networks are usually hierarchically configured, according to Cisco campus networks are formed of three layers:

- ***Core or Core layer:*** This layer uses a high-speed backbone; it is where all the accesses coming from the internet arrive, and it is where all the different sections of the network will be joined in a single network.

- ***Distribution Layer:*** The function of this layer is to control the flow of information in the access layer by routing between the VLANs that have been defined, allowing security policies to be implemented.

- ***Access Layer:*** The purpose of this layer is to allow the connection between the end devices (pc, laptop, printers, and smartphones) by providing a means of connection through switches and access points.

For security and confidentiality reasons, at present, they advise limiting the scope of broadcast traffic, so that an unauthorized user cannot access resources and information that does not belong to him.

For example, the corporate network, the financial and accounting departments, are generally in separate VLANs from the other users, since each of these groups deals with confidential information and each of the VLANs constitutes a broadcast domain. In this way, the communication between members of the same group can be done at level 2, and the groups are isolated from each other, they can only communicate through routes.

The definition of multiple VLANs and the use of trunk links, compared to LAN networks interconnected with a router, is a scalable solution. If you decide to create new groups, you can easily accommodate the new VLANs by redistributing the switch ports. In addition, the membership of a member of the corporation to a VLAN is independent of its physical location.

VLAN Related Commands in Cisco IOS

We present some of the commands that are most commonly used for the configuration of VLANs on switches and routers that use the Cisco IOS.

Creating new VLANs:

Switch> enable

```
Switch# configure terminal
Switch(config)# vlan 10
Switch(config-vlan)# name VLAN-ejemplo-10
Switch(config-vlan)# exit
Switch(config)# vlan 20
Switch(config-vlan)# name “VLAN ejemplo 20”
Switch(config-vlan)# exit
Switch(config)# vlan 30
Switch(config-vlan)# name  ejemplo30
Switch(config-vlan)# exit
```

Define a port as Trunk:

```
Switch(config)# interface gigabitEthernet 0/1
Switch(config-if)# switchport
Switch(config-if)# switchport mode trunk
Switch(config-if)# switchport trunk native VLAN 10
Switch(config-if)# switchport trunk allowed VLAN 20, 30
Switch(config-if)# exit
```

We define VLAN 10 as native VLAN and allow them to pass only from VLANs 10, 20, and 30.

Define a port as Access:

```
Switch> enable
Switch# configure terminal
Switch(config)# interface fastEthernet 0/1
Switch(config-if)# switchport
Switch(config-if)# switchport mode access
Switch(config-if)# switchport  access vlan 10
Switch(config-if)# exit
Switch(config)# interface fastEthernet 0/2
Switch(config-if)# switchport
Switch(config-if)# switchport mode access
Switch(config-if)# switchport  access vlan 20
Switch(config-if)# exit
Switch(config)# interface fastEthernet 0/3
Switch(config-if)# switchport
Switch(config-if)# switchport mode access
```

Switch(config-if)# switchport access vlan 30

Switch(config-if)# exit

Define subinterface on a Router:

Router > enable

Router # configure terminal

Router(config)# interface fastEthernet 0/1

Router(config-if)# no ip address

Router(config-if)# exit

Router(config)# interface fastEthernet 0/1.10

Router(config-if)# encapsulation dot1q 10 native

Router(config-if)# ip address 172.16.10.1 255.255.255.0

Router(config-if)# exit

Router(config)# interface fastEthernet 0/1.20

Router(config-if)# encapsulation dot1q 20

Router(config-if)# ip address 172.16.20.1 255.255.255.0

Router(config-if)# exit

Router(config)# interface fastEthernet 0/1.30

```
Router(config-if)# encapsulation dot1q 30

Router(config-if)# ip address 172.16.30.1 255.255.255.0

Router(config-if)# exit
```

This configuration allows the router to exchange data between VLANs.

Throughout this chapter, we have discussed the fundamentals of virtual local networks (VLANs), advantages, and features. In addition, examples have been provided as a basis for learning how to create and configure them.

To see what you've really learned about VLANs, it's time to get down to business and try to create, configure, and monitor them using supporting switches. That's how you learn best, plus you always have the help command, which also allows you to learn new aspects and go deeper into VLAN configuration.

Chapter Three

Routing Concept And Types

In today's corporate context of digital business transformation, relying on a high-performance Internet network is becoming increasingly critical for companies vying for market leadership. Therefore, maintaining a well-managed and secure network is a big challenge for many corporations that need to invest in intelligent, high-performance routing systems.

The basic definition of the internet is that it corresponds to a collection of interconnected networks, whereas routers can be defined as the intersection that connects these networks, that is, the points that make this bridge possible. Therefore, they are crucial instruments for the good performance of any process developed in the network.

The system that controls and manages a group of networks and routers is known as the Autonomous System, which defines the organization of routers hierarchically. More specifically, some routers are only used to exchange data between groups of networks controlled by the same administrative authority and routers that also communicate between administrative authorities.

Router and Routing - The Start

In this chapter about the router and its routing capability, let's start talking about static routing, and we're going to address dynamic routing protocols.

What is the Router?

The router, also known as a router, is a device whose main function is to send or route data packets from one network to another, that is, interconnect networks in layer 3. To this interconnection in layer 3, we commonly give the name of routing.

Router Operation

The basic operation of a Router, as we have already said, consists of sending the network packets along the most appropriate path or route at all times. So that you can do this work, the Router stores the received packets and processes the source and destination information they own.

Based on this information, it sends the packets to another router or to the final host, in an activity called 'routing.' Each Router is responsible for deciding the next hop based on its routing table.

What is Routing?

Routing is the most important form used on the Internet for the delivery of data packets between hosts (network equipment, generally including computers, routers, etc.). Its primary function, therefore, is to deliver consistent end-to-end packet delivery to applications or other protocol layers across an interconnected network infrastructure. To this end, routing performs communication path determination, packet switching over these paths, and route processing functions for a particular communication system.

In other words, for packets to be routed using message or packet switching, a route must be determined or chosen continuously. Determining and choosing this route is what was named as routing. The commonly used routing model is hop-by-hop, in which each router receives and opens a data packet, checks the destination address in the IP header, calculates the next hop it will leave the package one step closer to its destination and deliver the package in this next hop. This process repeats and continues until the package is delivered to its recipient.

The path determination function allows routers to select their most appropriate port for forwarding received packets. The routing service enables the router to analyze the available paths to a given destination and to establish the preferred path for sending packets to that destination. In this communication path determination, routing services perform:

- Initialization and maintenance of route tables;
- Route update processes and protocols;
- Specification of addresses and routing domains;
- Assignment and control of routing metrics.

Route information for packet propagation can be configured statically by the network administrator or collected through dynamic processes running on the network.

Routing Types

It is the function of searching for a path in a network for sending packages whose topologies have great connectivity. Since it is a question of finding the best possible route, the first thing will be to define what is meant by the best route (through administrative distance) and, consequently, what is the metric that should be used to measure it.

A router is a network device that allows packet routing between independent networks. This routing is done according to a set of rules that make up the routing table. Routing protocols are the set of rules used by a router when establishing communication with another router to share information, where such information is used for the creation of routing tables.

Static Routing

Static routes are defined administratively and establish specific routes to be followed by packets to pass from a source port to a destination port. This is how an accurate routing control is established according to the administrator's parameters.

Dynamic Routing

Dynamic routing allows routers to adjust the paths used to transmit IP packets. This can be done in real-time. Each protocol has its own methods to define routes (shortest path, use routes published in pairs, etc.).

Internal Routing Protocol

Routers used to exchange information within Autonomous Systems, common within organizations, are called interior routers and can use a variety of Interior Gateway Protocols (IGPs). These include RIP, IGRP, EIGRP, OSPF, and Integrated IS-IS, the latter being the most common.

Open Shortest Path First (OSPF)

This protocol was developed by the Internet Engineering Task Force (IETF). It is characterized by being a hierarchical intra-domain protocol based on the Link-State algorithm and was specifically designed to operate with large networks. Other features of the OSPF protocol are:

- The inclusion of the type of service routing (TOS) routing;

- Providing load balancing, which allows the administrator to specify multiple routes at the same cost to the same destination. OSPF distributes traffic evenly across all routes;
- Support for routes to specific hosts, subnets, and networks;
- The possibility of configuring a virtual network topology, regardless of the physical connection topology;
- Using small hello packets to verify link operation without having to transfer large tables.

Integrated Intermediate System to Intermediate System Routing Exchange Protocol (IS-IS)

IS-IS, like OSPF, is a hierarchical intra-domain protocol that uses the Link State algorithm. It can work over multiple subnets, including broadcasting to LANs, WANs, and peer-to-peer links. Integrated IS-IS, like other integrated routing protocols, calls all routers to use a single routing algorithm.

External Routing Protocol

Routers that exchange data between Autonomous Systems are called external routers, which use the Exterior Gateway Protocol (EGP) or BGP (Border Gateway Protocol). For this type of routing, collections of Classless Inter-Domain Routing (CIDR) prefixes identified by an Autonomous System number are considered.

Border Gateway Protocol (BGP)

It is characterized by being an interdomain routing protocol, created for use in the main internet routers. BGP is designed to prevent routing loops in arbitrary topologies, the most serious problem of its predecessor, Exterior Gateway Protocol (EGP).

Another problem that EGP does not solve - and is addressed by BGP is policy-based routing, a routing based on a set of non-technical rules defined by the Autonomous Systems. Already the latest version of BGP, BGP4, is designed to withstand the problems caused by the booming internet.

Routing in the OSI model

In the OSI model, different levels or layers are distinguished in which the machines can work and communicate to understand each other. As the elements that make up the network layer, routers have to take care of fulfilling the two main tasks assigned to it:

Packet Forwarding

When a packet reaches the inbound link of a router, it has to pass the packet to the appropriate outbound link. An important feature of the routers is that they do not broadcast diffusive traffic.

Packet Routing

Through the use of routing algorithms, you have to be able to determine the route that packets must follow as they flow from a sender to a receiver. Therefore, we must distinguish between forwarding and routing. Forwarding consists of picking up a package at the entrance and sending it through the output indicated in the table while routing means the process of making that table.

Switches vs. Routers

A switch, like a router, is also a switching device for storage and forwarding packets. The fundamental difference is that the switch operates in layer 2 (data link layer) of the OSI model, so that, to send a packet is based on a MAC address, unlike a router that uses the IP address. The other big difference is that routers switch packets in software and switches in hardware.

Router and Routing - Static Routes (Static Routing)

Static Routes or Static Routing are the simplest and least scalable ways to build a routing table. That said, what are the static routes, and how can we use them is what we will be dealing within this section. We take the second step in the direction of knowing the router and the way we do the Routing.

Routing

Let's understand a little more about routing or routing.

We can simply say that routing is the process that the router uses to decide where to send a packet. We can imagine the router as a center for handling mail letters. There they receive all the letters, separate according to their destination, and send them in the best way.

It also does the router, receives the packets, checks the route table that tells you which is the best way to send this packet. As we saw, the route table can be armed statically or dynamically, and we will understand how you can work statically. If you want to delve a little deeper into the route table, mark anywhere in this sentence, and we'll take you to an article about them.

Static Routes (Static Routing)

To understand static routes, we will use a small example, which we see in the image:

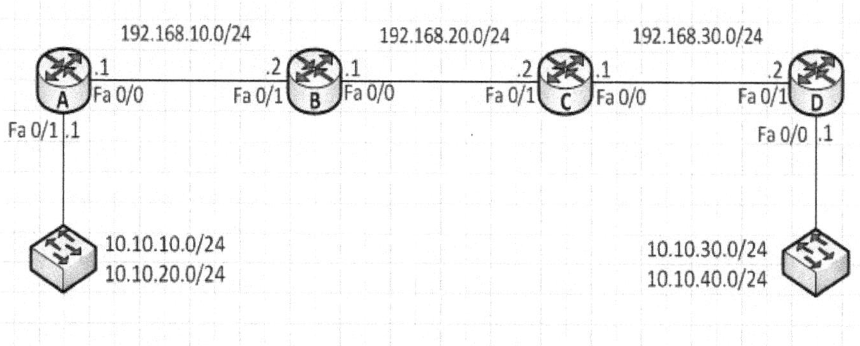

Let's analyze the network proposed above, and we have four routers, A, B, C, and D.

Among these four routers there are three networks / 24 that interconnect, they are:

192.168.10.0 / 24 - Between routers A and B

192.168.20.0 /24 – Entre the routers B and C

192.168.30.0 / 24 - Between the routers C and D

Then we see that there are two LAN networks connected to router A and two other LAN networks connected to router D.

Automatically each of the routers will know the networks that it has directly connected, so the routing tables would be:

Router A	Router B	Router C	Router D
192.168.10.0/24 by Fa 0/0	192.168.10.0/24 by Fa 0/1	192.168.20.0/24 by Fa 0/1	192.168.30.0/24 by Fa 0/1
10.10.10.0/24 by Fa 0/1	192.168.20.0/24 by Fa 0/0	192.168.30.0/24 by Fa 0/0	10.10.30.0/24 by Fa 0/0
10.10.20.0/24 by Fa 0/1			10.10.40.0/24 by Fa 0/0

Note that with the current routing tables, it is impossible for a host on the 10.10.10.0/24 network, to send a packet for a host on the 10.10.30.0/24 network.

This packet, when it reaches Router A, will be discarded, since Router A has no route to the 10.10.30.0/24 network. There we see an important concept: When the router has no route to the destination of a packet, it will directly discard it.

Now how will we do so that our friend from the 10.10.10.0/24 network can reach the 10.10.30.0/24 network?

We will create static routes for networks!

Let's not forget that to create static routes, and you have to have full knowledge of the network and routes have to be added manually all the way, which makes this solution not very scalable.

Well ... then we are going to create the routes so that networks 10.10.10.0/24 and 10.10.30.0/24 can exchange packages.

Let's look at the drawing once more:

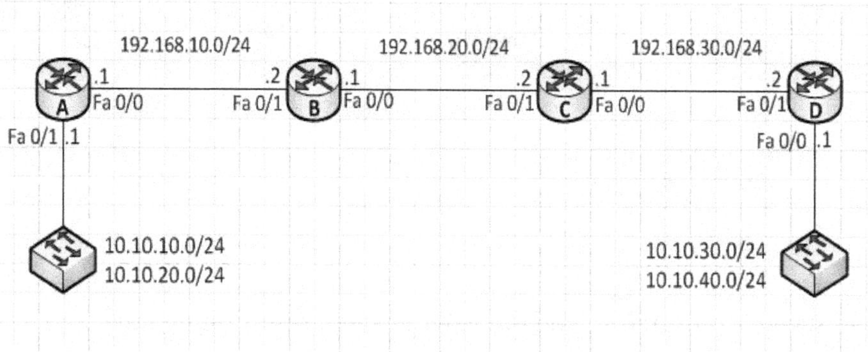

The question we have to ask is:

Where does the packet that arrives at router A have to exit, if we want it to reach the network 10.10.30.0/24?

The answer would be for the Fa 0/0 interface

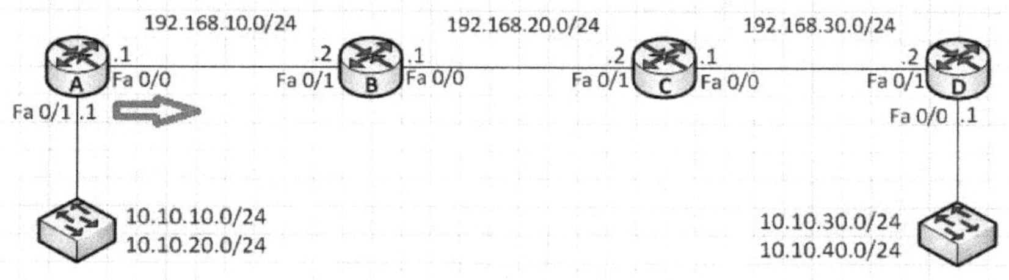

So we get to Router B, and we ask the same question again:

Where does the packet that arrives at Router B have to exit, if we want it to reach the network 10.10.30.0/24

The answer is the same, for the Fa 0/0 interface

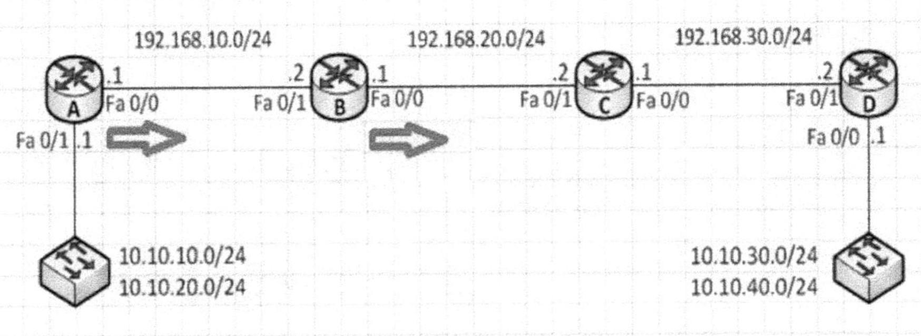

So we get to router C, and we ask the same question again:

Where does the packet that arrives at router C have to exit, if we want it to reach the network 10.10.30.0/24?

The answer again is the same, through the Fa 0/0 interface

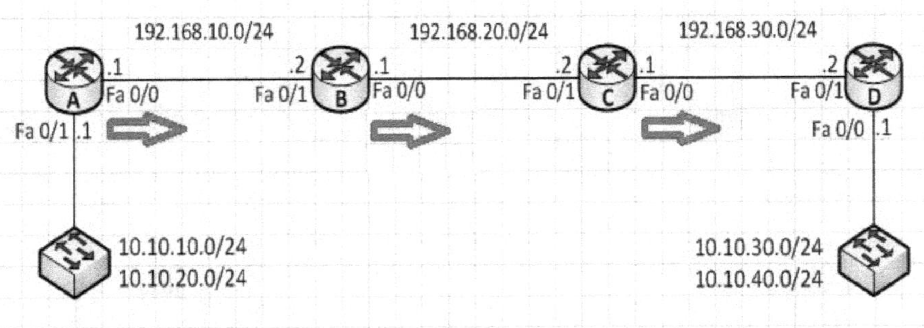

Note that it is a repetitive process, and it may seem obvious since, in the example, we have only one possible path.

Imagine the same in a network that is a bit more complex:

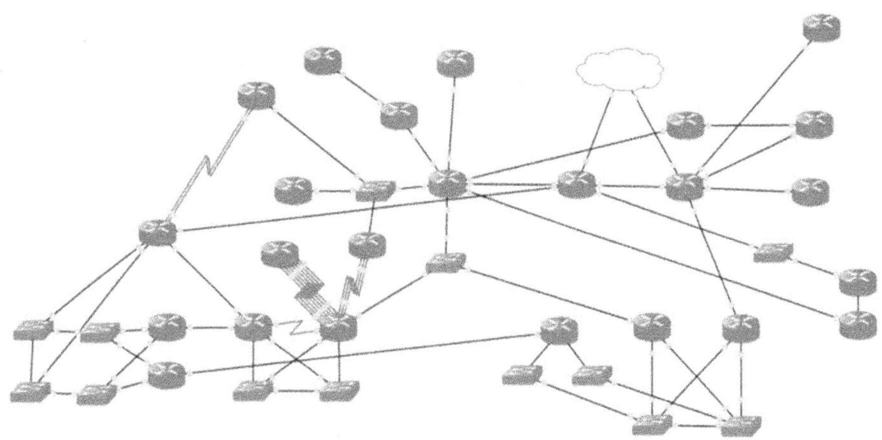

I think it is very clear because this static route model is not very scalable.

Let's continue with our example.

Finally, we reach router D, and there we already have the way to the 10.10.30.0/24 network since it is directly connected.

How is our route chart after that?

Let's see:

Router A	Router B	Router C	Router D
192.168.10.0/24 by Fa 0/0	192.168.10.0/24 by Fa 0/1	192.168.20.0/24 by Fa 0/1	192.168.30.0/24 by Fa 0/1
10.10.10.0/24 by Fa 0/1	192.168.20.0/24 by Fa 0/0	192.168.30.0/24 by Fa 0/0	10.10.30.0/24 by Fa 0/0
10.10.20.0/24 by Fa 0/1	**10.10.30.0/24 by Fa 0/0**	**10.10.30.0/24 by Fa 0/0**	10.10.40.0/24 by Fa 0/0
10.10.30.0/24 by Fa 0/0			

Perfect, we reach the destination network, now so that we can receive an answer, the reverse path must be done.

The answer comes through router D, let's ask our question again:

Where does the packet that arrives at router D have to exit, if we want it to reach the network 10.10.10.0/24?

The answer is that you have to exit through the Fa 0/1 interface

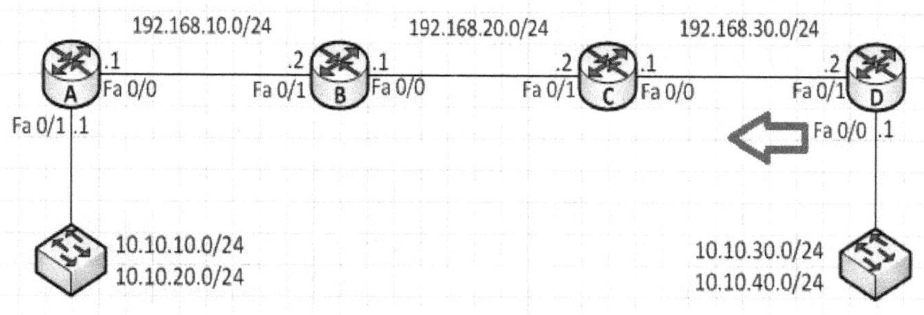

Perfect, we reach the destination network, now so that we can receive an answer, the reverse path must be done.

The answer comes through router D, let's ask again our question:

Where does the packet that arrives at router D have to exit, if we want it to reach the network 10.10.10.0/24?

The answer is that you have to exit through the Fa 0/1 interface

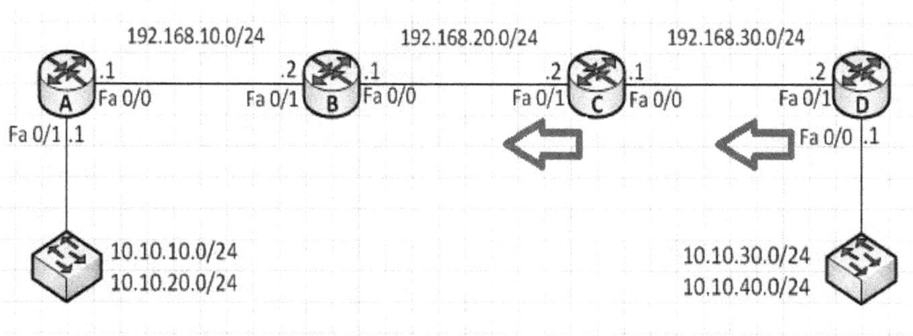

So we get to Router B, and we ask the same question again:

Where does the packet that arrives at router B have to exit, if we want it to reach the network 10.10.10.0/24?

The answer is the same again, through the Fa 0/1 interface

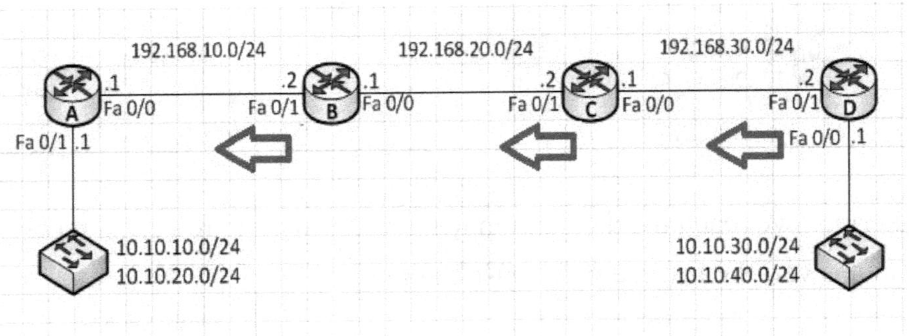

Finally, we reach the router A once again, and there we already have the way to the 10.10.10.0/24 network, which is directly connected.

Now, how is our route chart after that?

Let's see:

Router A	**Router B**	**Router C**	**Router D**
192.168.10.0/24	192.168.10.0/24	192.168.20.0/24	192.168.30.0/24
by Fa 0/0	by Fa 0/1	by Fa 0/1	by Fa 0/1
10.10.10.0/24	192.168.20.0/24	192.168.30.0/24	10.10.30.0/24
by Fa 0/1	by Fa 0/0	by Fa 0/0	by Fa 0/0

10.10.20.0/24	10.10.30.0/24	10.10.30.0/24	10.10.40.0/24
by Fa 0/1	by Fa 0/0	by Fa 0/0	by Fa 0/0
10.10.30.0/24	**10.10.10.0/24**	**10.10.10.0/24**	**10.10.10.0/24**
by Fa 0/0	**by Fa 0/1**	**by Fa 0/1**	**by Fa 0/1**

Now the 10.10.10.0/24 and 10.10.30.0/24 networks are fully connected, and any host that belongs to one of the two networks will be able to talk to a host on the other network without problems.

Static Routes in Practice

Let's see now what commands we would have to apply on the four routers so that our example can work.

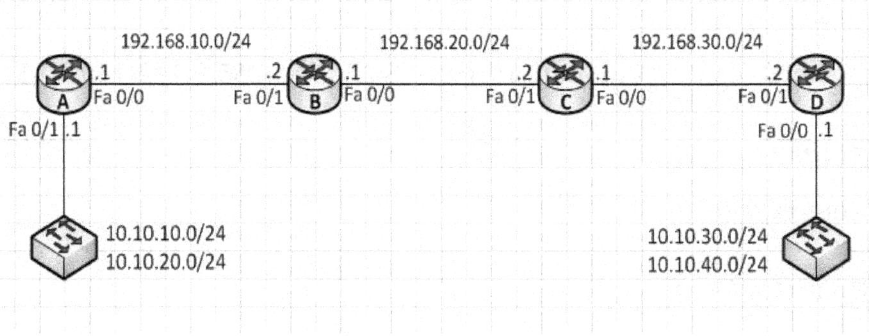

Router A

RouterA# enable

RouterA# Configure Terminal

RouterA (config)# ip route 10.10.30.0 255.255.255.0 192.168.10.2

10.10.30.0 is the IP of the destination network

255.255.255.0 in the netmask for the destination network (equivalent to / 24 in CIDR notation)

192.168.10.2 is the IP where the packet has to be sent (equivalent to Fa 0/0, it is the IP of the Fa 0/1 port of Router B)

Router B

RouterB# enable

RouterB# Configure Terminal

RouterB (config)# ip route 10.10.30.0 255.255.255.0 192.168.20.2

RouterB (config)# ip route 10.10.10.0 255.255.255.0 192.168.10.1

Router C

RouterC# enable

RouterC# Configure Terminal

RouterC (config)# ip route 10.10.30.0 255.255.255.0 192.168.30.2

RouterC (config)# ip route 10.10.10.0 255.255.255.0 192.168.20.1

Router D

RouterD# enable

RouterD# Configure Terminal

RouterD (config)# ip route 10.10.10.0 255.255.255.0 192.168.30.1

Packet Tracer, the New from an Old Acquaintance

The Cisco Packet Tracer is a simulation program that allows you to simulate a virtual network. It lets you configure a wide variety of devices such as routers, computers, switches, etc. From static IP addresses to hardware changes, Cisco Packet Tracer enables a variety of settings.

There are other good network simulators, and everyone has their preferences, but no other simulator that is as didactic as the Packet Tracer, the way you can visualize the network as a whole greatly helps those who are starting to have greater visibility on the operation of the network, even over all layers of the OSI model and not only the lower ones.

Features of Packet Tracer

Packet Tracer runs on Mac OS, Linux, and Windows. There is also a similar Android app. The program allows users to create different topologies and to build them with different network devices. A connection between the different devices is represented by the cable tool, which also supports different protocol types.

This not suitable for simulating production networks, even because the conception of the program is to be used for laboratory simulations of CCNA and CCNP students.

The Real Work

Now I propose that you can be putting into practice everything we saw and you can create static routes for the 10.10.20.0/24 and 10.10.40.0/24.

You can see how our route table will look after adding the new networks, as well as the commands that we have to apply on the four routers for everything to work.

Those who want can also apply all the information to replicate this model in the Packet Tracer.

Router and Routing - Dynamic Routing

Dynamic routes are very practical and have great scalability; in these two small advantages is everything that made dynamic routes a standard when we talk about data routing.

This is the topic we are going to discuss in this section. I am sure that at the end of this section you will be able to rest assured that this is the best way to have routes.

Now that in this big chapter, you could already learn what routing is coming, and then you know the static routes. Now you will learn about dynamic routes, a whole new world that includes the best-known protocols in the market. Start with the RIP, but you will also be learning OSPF and EIGRP.

Dynamic Routing

Before in static routing, what did I do? He went to each of the routers in the network and told him where to send the packets that arrive at each of the networks.

I just decided which is the best way, and the router only does what I indicated. When we try dynamic routing, it is the router that will make its own decision for each network.

I now delegate this task to a protocol that will decide the best path. Now, the question that surely occurs to you is: How does a protocol decide the best path?

Good...

There are several ways to do it, and each of the different protocols has its own way. We can even classify the protocols according to how they make this decision.

Let's learn a little more about how this classification works.

The Types of Decision

There are currently three different ways that a dynamic routing protocol can decide where to send a packet. We can also say that there are three different ways to measure the distance to a network.

The three ways are Distance Vector, Link State, and Hybrid. Let's talk a little about each of them so that we can identify their differences.

Distance Vector

The routing protocols, called Distance Vector or Distance Vector, have the concept that the network is a vector. When at some point in your life, you imagined a vector, it was always a line with a sense and a direction.

Well, in geometry classes, we see that the line is composed of several points.

Each of these points is a different router. So our vector is something like this:

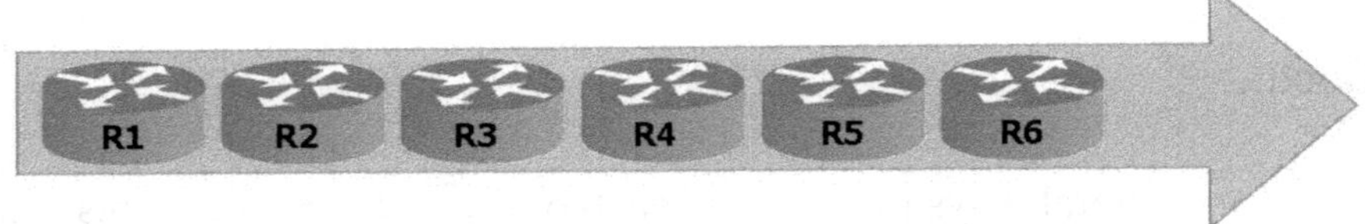

We know that if we are on router R1 and we want to reach router R4, we have to jump through R2 and R3.

This is how vector distance protocols work, and each router is a leap. Imagine now a slightly more complex scenario.

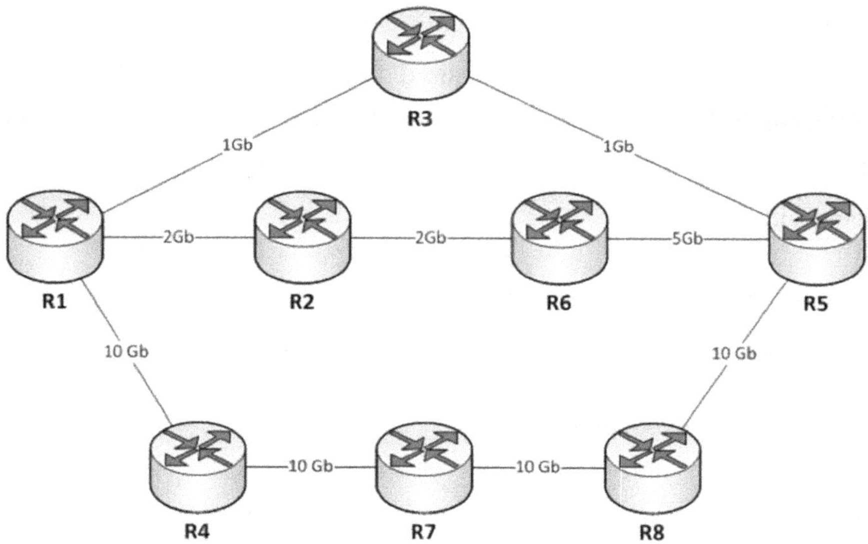

Now, if I want to leave router R1 to router R5, what path does a distance-vector protocol indicate? See that this example has several paths, with different jumps and speeds.

Let's change the question, in your opinion, as a future network administrator, which is the best way? What is your answer? The one with the most bandwidth? The one with the least jumps?

Later I answer what I think.

The vector distance protocol has a simple line of thinking. For him, the best way is the one with the least amount of jumps.

In this case, even if the path that goes through R4 has more bandwidth, our protocol will decide for R3, since there is only one jump. The protocol we know works in this way is RIP, in any of its two versions.

Link State

The link-state protocols understand that the modern network has different links and tries to improve the way of making decisions. These protocols evaluate the link between the routers by their bandwidth.

So each of the speeds is represented by a cost. The lower the cost to reach a network, the better the way is considered.

Let's look at the cost chart.

Speed	**Cost**
4 Mbps	250
10 Mbps	100
16 Mbps	62
100 Mbps	19
1 Gbps	4
2 Gbps	3
10 Gbps	2
100 Gbps	1

There we have the most common costs, and for our example, we are going to add one.

5 Gbps	2,5

Let's go back to our example.

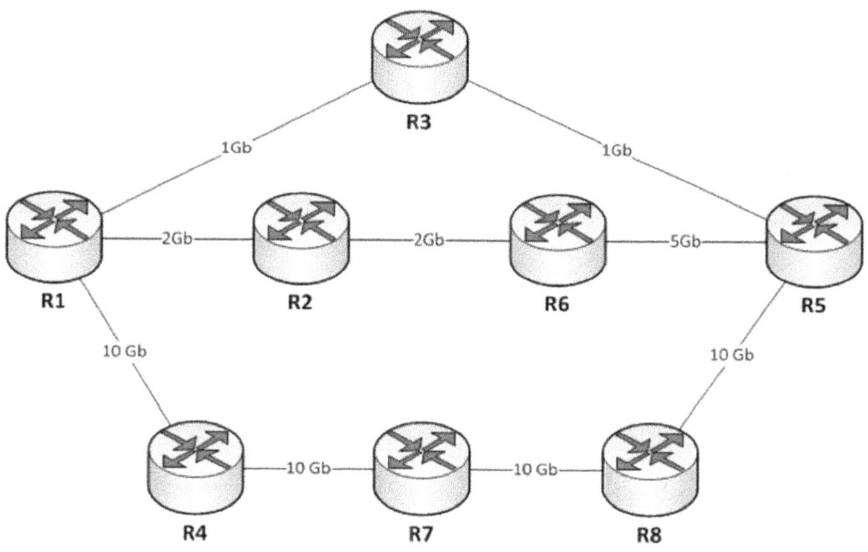

Now, if I want to leave router R1 to router R5, what path will a link-state protocol indicate?

The correct answer is the path by R4 - R7 - R8. Let's understand why this is the answer.

If we go through R3, we have two 1 Gb links that, according to our table, have cost 4.

If we go through R2 - R6, we have two links of 2 Gb and one link of 5 Gb, here what we are going to do is take the value of the smallest bandwidth.

While the part of the road has a cost of 2.5, this road as a whole has a cost 3.

If we go on the road through R4 - R7 - R8, we have four links of 10 Gb, so we have a cost of 2.

We know that link-state protocols will always decide for the lowest cost.

The lowest cost value we have is 2, and this was the path used.

Now I answer the question I asked before.

Do you remember? I asked: in your opinion, as a future network administrator, which is the best way?

In my opinion, the best way is where there is more bandwidth available. Understand, even if the link has 10 Gb of bandwidth, yes, at this moment, I have 9 Gb of this full width, and the other two links have no traffic.

Where our package would arrive faster ...

Surely on the road R2 - R6.

Understanding that, we see that while the link states are quite good, they are not yet perfect.

Examples of link status protocols are OSPF and IS-IS.

OBS: While EIGRP in many kinds of literature is classified as a link-state protocol, for Cisco, it is a hybrid protocol, so we will treat it as such. Personally, I think that EIGRP goes beyond a link-state protocol.

Hybrid (hybrids)

Now we come to the last type of dynamic routing protocol, the hybrid. Thus, protocols that use more than one measure to define their costs are classified.

The fact of using several measures in its calculation for cost makes these protocols much more precise. It also makes the path you are going to change according to the parameters you are using.

The best examples of hybrid protocols are EIGRP and BGP. In the case of EIGRP, the cost is calculated using the formula:

EIGRP cost = 256 * ((K1 * Bw) + (K2 * Bw) / (256-Load) + K3 * Delay) * (K5 / (Reliability + K4)))

The Ks are binary, so they can be 1 or 0.

Seeing this, we know that when I have them with 1, they are considered for cost, and when I have them with 0, we will not consider them.

When we talk about EIGRP, we will be detailing this formula further. Now the important thing is that they understand the concept of hybrid.

Advantages and Disadvantages of Dynamic Routing

Finally, let's talk a little about the advantages and disadvantages of having dynamic routing. By understanding their advantages, we will understand why dynamic routing protocols dominate modern networks.

Advantages of Dynamic Routing

- The main advantage of dynamic routing is to allow the network administrator to manage and configure their routes very easily.
- This facility allows the administrator to focus on other more important issues, especially when we deal with large networks.
- They already reflect the second advantage, which is scalability.
- The ability to grow the network quickly and efficiently.
- Surely these two advantages make us almost always use dynamic routing protocols.
- Another important point is the disadvantages, and in the end, if they were greater, it would not compensate for their use.

Disadvantages of Dynamic Routing

The disadvantages of dynamic routing are negligible in relation to its advantages. We highlight the two most important. The case that the routers exchange signaling is the first. Today there are still network links that are quite small, and losing part of your traffic capacity with signaling is a price to pay.

The second disadvantage is having to process the routes and the signals that arrive, make the router use more of its CPU. Both disadvantages were already a major problem, every day, and technology improves, and we have better CPU and bandwidth.

The OSI Model

The OSI model is undoubtedly the origin of all the standards we use for communication between hardware and software. All of us, at some point, already heard of him; it was not always like that.

Let's start from the beginning and understand the OSI model.

OSI Model: The Story that Changed Networks

Long ago, computers from different manufacturers did not recognize each other over the network, which caused many problems. Imagine a great company that had all the servers of an X brand. Acquire another smaller company with servers of a Y brand.

For the servers of the two companies to communicate, the Y brand servers had to be changed to X brand servers and companie began pressuring the government for money.

In turn, governments pressured the International Organization for Standardization (ISO) for a reference model. That is why in 1984, the International Organization for Standardization published its standard.

The Open Systems Interconnect model, also known as the OSI Model (ISO / IEC 7498-1).

OSI Model: A Seven Level or Seven Layer Model

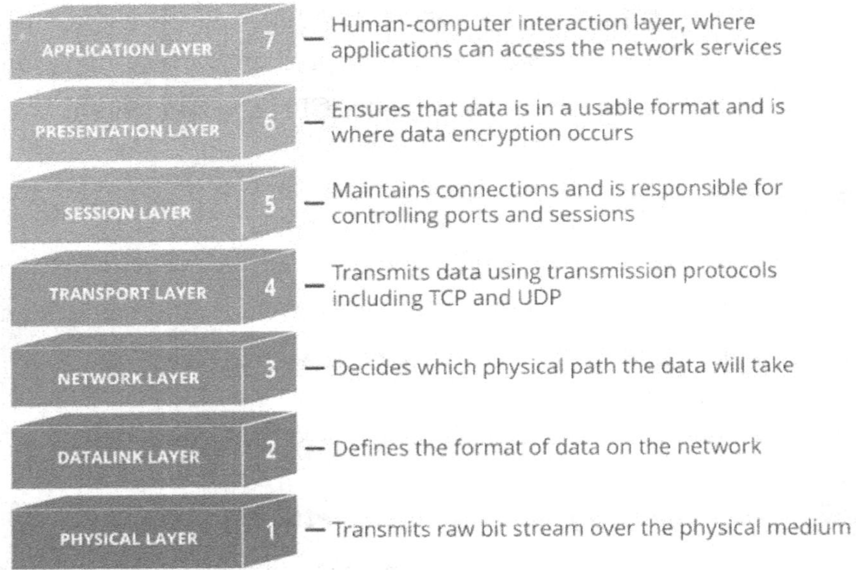
APPLICATION LAYER
7
— Human-computer interaction layer, where applications can access the network services
PRESENTATION LAYER
6
— Ensures that data is in a usable format and is where data encryption occurs
SESSION LAYER
5
— Maintains connections and is responsible for controlling ports and sessions
TRANSPORT LAYER
4
— Transmits data using transmission protocols including TCP and UDP
NETWORK LAYER
3
— Decides which physical path the data will take
DATALINK LAYER
2
— Defines the format of data on the network
PHYSICAL LAYER
1
— Transmits raw bit stream over the physical medium

The universal communication model was defined, and it worked with seven different levels. These levels have to do with the different levels of software and hardware that existed at that time.

And what are the seven levels?

In general, the data flow is made from the highest layer to the lowest layer. It is in this way, and we will follow the flow.

The Layers of the OSI Model

Seventh Level - Application Level or Layer

The application layer is the layer of the OSI model closest to the user; for this reason, it is also the level that has the largest number of existing protocols since users are the ones with a large number of needs.

This level is responsible for converting the differences that exist between the various operating and application systems for a standard, that is, this litter receives the information that comes from the user we call SDU (Service Data Unit) and adds the control information we call from PCI (Protocol Control Information) so that we have as output the well-known PDU (Protocol Data Unit).

The best-known protocols of this layer are NFS, AFP, HTTP, SMTP, FTP, SSH, Telnet, SIP, RDP, IRC, SNMP, NNTP, POP3, IMAP, BitTorrent, DNS, among others.

Sixth Level - Presentation Level or Layer

It is an intermediate layer between the session and application. It is responsible that the information can be sent in a way that the recipient can understand. It deals with aspects such as the semantics and syntax of the transmitted data.

For example, the conversion so that protocols such as tcp / ip can talk to ipx / spx. This layer also allows you to encrypt and compress data.

For example, the conversion of ASCII data to EBCDIC. Data cryptography is also done in this layer. Therefore, it could be said that this layer acts as a universal translator.

Fifth Level - Session Level or layer

This layer is responsible for maintaining and controlling the link established between two computers that are transmitting data of any kind.

To obtain success in the communication process, the session layer has to worry about synchronization between hosts, so that the open session between them stays up.

The best-known protocols of this layer are SMTP, FTP, SAP, SSH, ZIP, RCP, SCP, Netbios, ASP, among others.

Fourth Level - Transport Level or Layer

The transport layer ensures that messages reach their recipient without errors, in the correct sequence, and without data loss. Upper layer protocols have no concern about data transfer. It is also this layer that is responsible for receiving the data sent by the session layer.

After fragmenting them to be sent to the network layer, at the reception, it does the reverse process, putting the packets sent by the network layer into segments for the session layer.

The Importance of the Transport Layer

- The transport layer separates the application level layers (layers 5 through 7) from the physical level layers (layers 1 through 3). This layer communicates between these two groups and determines the kind of service needed.

- The service class can be connection-oriented.
- With error control and confirmation service of packet reception (TCP).
- The service class may also not be connection-oriented.
- Without all error controls and packet reception (UDP).

The hardware and/or software that is inside the transport layer communicates with its users through the service rules that are exchanged through one or more TSAP (Transport Service Access Point), which are managed according to the type of service provided.

These rules are transported by the TPDU (Transport Protocol Data Unit). The size and complexity of a transport protocol will depend on the type of service that it can obtain in the network layer, that is, in a network layer that can make transport with more confidence with virtual circuit capacity, a Minimum transport layer is necessary.

If the network layer is not very reliable or if it only has datagram support, the transport protocol will have to include external error detection and recovery tasks.

Modes of Transport Protocols

The ISO defines that transport protocols can operate in two modes:

- Connection-oriented - As an example of a protocol that is connection-oriented, we have TCP.

- Not connection-oriented - As an example of a protocol that is not connection-oriented, we have UDP.

I think it is quite clear that transport protocols that are not connection-oriented are not reliable since they do not guarantee the delivery of TPDUs, nor the ordering of them.

Still, in structures where the service of the network layer, and the lower two, is quite reliable, as in local networks or data centers, a transport protocol that is not connection-oriented is usually used, more than anything to reduce the overhead of connection-oriented protocols.

Classes of the Transport Layer

The functions implemented by the transport layer are directly related to the desired service quality; with this thought, five kinds of connection-oriented protocols were created:

- Class 0: it is the simplest of all, there is no error detection and recovery mechanism;

- Class 1: in this class, only the recovery of basic errors signaled by the network is made;

- Class 2: This class allows several transport connections to be multiplexed above a single network connection, it can also implement flow control mechanisms;

- Class 3: in this class, we can define the recovery of the errors signaled by the network and that several transport connections are multiplexed above a network connection;
- Class 4: This class allows error detection and recovery to be configured and also that several transport connections are multiplexed on top of a single network connection.

The best-known protocols of this layer are TCP, UDP, ZIP, NBP, IPX / SPX.

Pause for Important Information: Layers that go from one End to the Other End

The layers we saw so far are layers that range from origin to destination or from end-to-end. These upper layers do not consider the details of the underlying resources.

The software in the transport, session, presentation, and application layers are usually on the source host. These upper layers speak directly to similar software on the destination host.

They use a special sequence of bits. This sequence is at the beginning and end of the initial flow of bits and control messages.

The lower layers that we are going to detail look at all the subparts of the path independently. The closer to the physical layer, in greater detail.

Thus, in the same number of parts, the same plot can be divided between origin and destination.

Retaking with the OSI Model Layers: Third Level - Network Level or Layer

The network layer provides the functional and procedural means for transferring variable size data into sequences, from an origin on a host that is in a data network to a destination host that is on a network of different data, trying to maintain the quality of service that would have been required by the transport layer.

The devices that facilitate this task are called routers or routers, although it is more frequent to find it with the English name routers. Routers work in this layer, although they can act as a level 2 switch in certain cases, depending on the function assigned to it.

Firewalls act primarily on this layer, to discard machine addresses. The network layer does the routing of functions, and can also fragment and reassemble data. They can also send reports of package delivery errors.

"Thanks to the functions that routers perform, it is possible that the existence of the internet is possible."

This layer can be divided into three sub-layers:

- Access sub layer - protocols that work directly with the network interface, such as X.25, are considered for this sublayer;
- Convergence dependent sub layer - this sublayer is necessary to raise the level of a traffic network, to the level of a network at each end;

- Independent convergence sub layer - this sublayer is for transferring across multiple networks. It controls the operation of sub-networks, packet routing, congestion control, charging, and makes it possible for heterogeneous networks to be interconnected.

The best-known protocols of this layer are IP, IPX / SPX, X.25, APPLETALK, RIP, IGRP, EIGRP, OSPF, BGP, IS-IS, among others.

The Second Level - Level or Data Link Layer

The data link layer provides reliable data transit through a physical link. This allows the layers above it to be sure that the transmission of data through the physical link is going to be done practically without errors.

This layer deals with physical addressing, access to the environment, error detection, orderly distribution of frames, and flow control. It is one of the most important aspects to review when connecting two computers.

Since it is between layers 1 and 3 as an essential part for the creation of its basic protocols to regulate the shape of the connection between computers, thus determining the passage of frames.

Frame = unit of measurement of the information in this layer, which is nothing more than the segmentation of the data using packets.

It is important to maintain an excellent adaptation to the physical environment (the most used are the UTP cable, twisted pair or 8-wire, and the optical fiber, multimode and single-mode), with the network medium that redirects the connections through a router.

The device that uses the link layer is the Switch. The Switch is responsible for receiving the router data and sending each of these to their respective recipients:

- servers.
- computers.
- IP phones
- mobile phones.
- Printers
- tablets
- Different devices with network access.

Sub Levels of the Data Link Layer

The link level is divided into two sub-levels:

- Higher Sub Level - Logical Link Control (LLC) - The LLC protocol can be used over all IEEE protocols of the MAC sub-level, such as IEEE 802.3 (Ethernet), IEEE 802.4 (Token Bus) and IEEE 802.5 (Token Ring). He hides the differences between the protocols of the MAC sub-level. The LLC is used when it is necessary to achieve flow control or reliable communication;

- Lower sub-level - media access control (MAC - Medium Access Control) has some important protocols, such as IEEE 802.3 (Ethernet), IEEE 802.4 (Token Bus), and IEEE 802.5 (Token Ring). The higher-level protocol may or may not use the LLC sub-level, depending on the expected reliability for that level.

The best-known protocols of this layer are ARP, PPP, LAPB, SLIP, SDLC, HDLC, LAPD, Frame Relay, IEEE, among others.

First Level - Level or Physical Layer

The physical layer defines the electrical, mechanical, procedural, and functional specifications. To activate, maintain, and deactivate the physical link between end systems.

Its main functions can be summarized as:

- Define the physical means or means by which the communication will travel: twisted pair cable (or not, as in RS232 / EIA232), coaxial cable, waveguides, air, fiber optics.

- Define the material (mechanical components and connectors) and electrical (voltage levels) characteristics that will be used in the transmission of data by physical means.

- Define the functional characteristics of the interface (establishment, maintenance, and release of the physical link).

- Transmitting the bitstream through the media.

- Handle the electrical signals of the transmission medium, poles in an outlet, etc.

- Guarantee the connection (although not the reliability of said connection).

The physical layer is also responsible for defining whether or not the transmission can be performed simultaneously in both directions. The best-known protocols of this layer are IEE 1394, DLS, ISDN, Bluetooth, GSM, USB, ADSL, among others.

The objective of the OSI model is to provide a common basis. That allows the coordinate development of standards for the interconnection of systems. Look that the open term does not apply to any particular technology, implementation, or interconnection.

If it applies to the adoption of standards for the exchange of information, standards that represent a functional analysis of any communication process, the development of the OSI model represented an effort in the attempt to achieve a standard.

For the development of new technologies for the implementation of network products, which were compatible with each other, the OSI model is conceptual and not a real implementation architecture of network protocols.

Routing Protocols

Computer networks use hardware devices called routers or routers to transmit data between networks. To carry out this task, the router must be configured with a routing protocol. Some examples of protocols include Open Shortest Path First (OSPF), Border Gateway Protocol (BGP), and Routing Information Protocol (RIP). The routing protocol tells the router how to learn about other routers in a network and build routing tables that identify where each network is located.

Routing protocols include the Internet Protocol (IP), the most widely used routed protocol, and Internetwork Packet Exchange (IPX), which Novell Corporation uses within its network operating system. The IP protocol is represented by a numerical address that is in a decimal format with dots. When using IP version 4 as an example, this address is 32 bits long.

An IP address consists of the network address, which identifies a network in an autonomous system, and the server address, which identifies a server device, like a computer.

Classes of Routing Protocols

Routing protocols include link status, distance vector, and hybrid class types. The OSPF routing protocol is within the type of link status class, which calculates the shortest route between the source and destination networks. The RIP routing protocol is a distance-vector class type, and the best path is deterministic based on the least number of hops from one router to another. A hybrid protocol can have characteristics of both a link-state and distance vector protocol. An example would be the Cisco Enhanced Interior Gateway Routing (EIGRP) protocol.

Autonomous systems: Autonomous is a term used to describe a system that includes all computers and local area networks that fall within an administrative domain contained in a wide area network. If Company X has five buildings with a local area network of computers in each building and uses routers to establish a wide area network connection between the buildings, the global network would be considered an autonomous system.

Most routing algorithms belong to one of these two features:

- Vectordistance.
- Link status.

Vector distance: Protocols distance vector routing. Routing protocols distance-vector periodic copies of the routing tables of a router to another. Routing algorithms based on distance vector algorithms are also known as Bellman-Ford. Routing protocols vector- distance:

Link status: Routing protocols link-state maintains a complex database, with information on the network topology. Algorithms link state, also known as algorithms Dijkstra's or SPF ("first route shorter"). The distance vector algorithm provides undetermined information about distant networks and no information about distant routers.

Points of interest about the status of the link:

- Load on the processor.
- Memory requirements.
- Use of the bandwidth.

Distance Vector vs. Link State

Distance vector	**Link Status**
displays the topology from net since the perspective neighbors	You get a common view of the topology of the entire network.
Add the distance vector from router to router	Calculate the shortest route to other routers
Makes updates periodic with frequency and convergence is slow	Offers updates unchained by events with a faster convergence
Send copies of the routing tables to neighboring routers	Send updates link-state routing to other routers
Use a flat topology	It allows the design hierarchical for big internetworks

RIPV2 (distance vector)

RIP stands for Routing Information Protocol (Routing Information Protocol). Is a protocol gateway link internal or IGP (Interior Gateway Protocol) used by routers (routers) to exchange information about IP networks that are connected?

Its routing algorithm is based on distance vector and calculates the metric or route short as possible to the destination from the number of "hops" or intermediate devices that IP packets must traverse.

The maximum hop limit in RIP is 15, so that the reach 16 considers a path unattainable or undesirable. Unlike other protocols, RIP protocol is a free, i.e., that can be used by different router and not just by a single owner.

- UDP uses port 520
- Classless protocol (supports CIDR)
- supports VLSMs
- The metric is the number of hops (the number of routers that a packet must travel through before reaching its destination.)
- periodic routing updates are sent every 30 seconds to the address 224.0.0.9 multicast
- 25 routes per message RIP (24 if authentication is used).
- Supports authentication.

- Split Horizon with Poison implements reverse.
- Implements update events.
- The subnet mask is included.
- The administrative distance is 120.
- Use in small networks (flat networks) or to the edge of large networks

Let's set the RIPV2 protocol on our network, and we will make a small simulation operation.

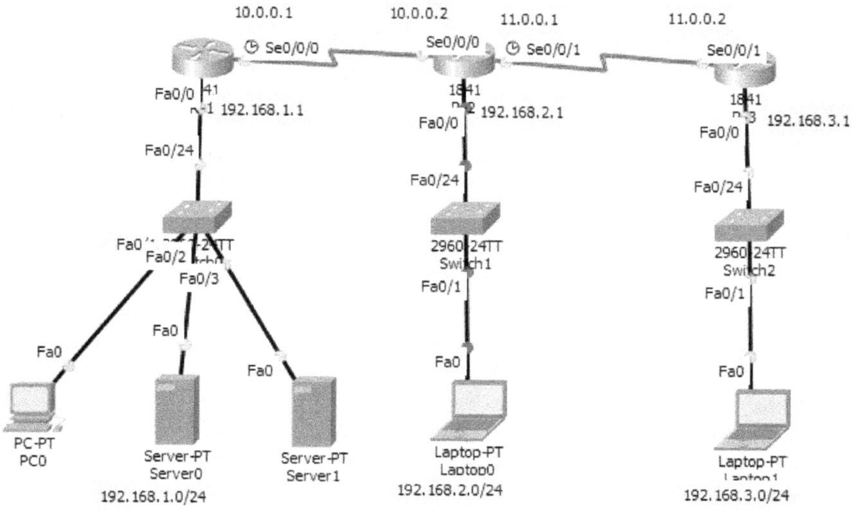

Let's set the RIPV2 protocol for a set of routers that are at the bottom of the network as an example to demonstrate the operation of the protocol and its configuration.

Access the command line of the router "ETSINF" and launched the following commands configuration mode:

> ETSINF (conf-t) # router rip→ We enable the protocol rip
>
> ETSINF (conf-t) # version 2→ activate version 2 of the protocol.
>
> ETSINF (router-rip) # network [network directly connected] →The IP address of the networks to which the router is directly connected.

NOTE: In this case, we must be vigilant and also publishes a network of Vlan what they are directly connected in the Vlan's.

Throwing the # show ip route command → we can see the routing table, and it should be like this:

```
R2#show ip route
Codes: L - local, C - connected, S - static, R - RIP, M - mobile, B - BGP
       D - EIGRP, EX - EIGRP external, O - OSPF, IA - OSPF inter area
       N1 - OSPF NSSA external type 1, N2 - OSPF NSSA external type 2
       E1 - OSPF external type 1, E2 - OSPF external type 2, E - EGP
       i - IS-IS, L1 - IS-IS level-1, L2 - IS-IS level-2, ia - IS-IS inter area
       * - candidate default, U - per-user static route, o - ODR
       P - periodic downloaded static route

Gateway of last resort is 0.0.0.0 to network 0.0.0.0

     172.17.0.0/16 is variably subnetted, 9 subnets, 4 masks
O       172.17.0.0/24 [110/782] via 172.17.123.6, 00:09:26, Serial0/0/1
O IA    172.17.1.1/32 [110/7501] via 172.17.123.1, 00:09:26, Serial0/0/0
O IA    172.17.2.1/32 [110/7501] via 172.17.123.1, 00:09:26, Serial0/0/0
O IA    172.17.3.1/32 [110/7501] via 172.17.123.1, 00:09:26, Serial0/0/0
O IA    172.17.4.0/22 [110/782] via 172.17.123.6, 00:09:26, Serial0/0/1
C       172.17.123.0/30 is directly connected, Serial0/0/0
L       172.17.123.2/32 is directly connected, Serial0/0/0
C       172.17.123.4/30 is directly connected, Serial0/0/1
L       172.17.123.5/32 is directly connected, Serial0/0/1
     209.165.200.0/24 is variably subnetted, 2 subnets, 2 masks
C       209.165.200.224/29 is directly connected, Loopback0
L       209.165.200.225/32 is directly connected, Loopback0
S*   0.0.0.0/0 is directly connected, Loopback0
R2#
```

Routes represented with "C" are directly connected routes, and routes represented with "R" are known routes from the RIPV2 protocol.

THE OSPF (link-state)

OSPF is a routing protocol called Link State using specific packages to meet that state. Such information packets are called LSAs (link state advertisements) and are sent to all routers within the area where you are working. Information on connected interfaces, metrics used, and other variables specific to a routing protocol is included in LSAs.

OSPF routers accumulate this link status information and use the SPF algorithm to calculate the shortest path to each node. As protocol keeps track of the status of links in the network, OSPF contrasts with other protocols (RIP, as mentioned above) is that existing are distance vector. Routers running distance vector algorithms send all or part of their routing tables in update messages to their neighbors.

Unlike other routing systems, OSPF can operate within a hierarchy. The largest entity within a hierarchy is what we call the self-contained system, which was explained in the previous section on routing protocols. As a quick explanation, an autonomous system (AS) is a group of networks under a common administration that share a routing strategy.

The OSPF protocol is internal to the AS, although capable of receiving and sending routes to other autonomous systems. An autonomous system can be divided into several areas, which are groups of contiguous networks with connected equipment (computers, servers, etc.). Routers with multiple interfaces can participate in multiple areas. These routers, which are called ABR (border routers in the area), maintain separate topological databases for each area.

For example, in a university network, we need to simulate an OSPF Meshing for the operation of the protocol. The protocol is responsible for border routers to interconnect the various faculties.

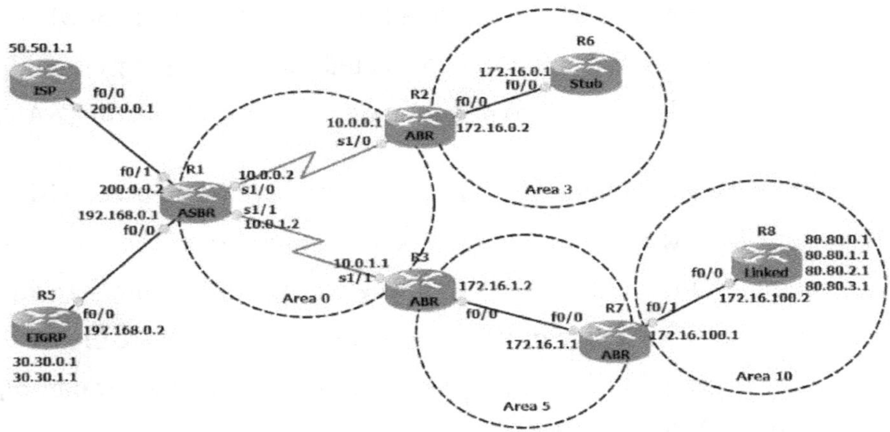

Let's set the OSPF protocol on the router "CPD2" access the command line configuration mode and launch the following commands:

Router (config) #router ospf 1

Router (config-router) #network [network address] wildcard [address wildcard] area [num]

Router (config-router) #network 172.16.0.72 0.0.0.3 area 0

Router (config-router) #network 172.16.0.76 0.0.0.3 area 0

Router (config-router) #network 172.16.0.48 0.0.0.3 area 0

Router (config-router) #network 172.16.0.44 0.0.0.3 area 0

What we do is in the router "Cpd2" OSPF routing activate "num" the number of process and then publish the networks to which is directly connected. This configuration has to be made on all routers in the mesh.

The configuration is basically similar to that of the RIPv2 protocol. Unlike the OSPF protocol, reacts when there is a change in the network, again restoring their routes in search of all paths.

OSPF Authentication Protocol

We will implement the authentication protocol between each OSPF network link, and we will make an example between the router "Cpd2" and its link with the "house of the student."

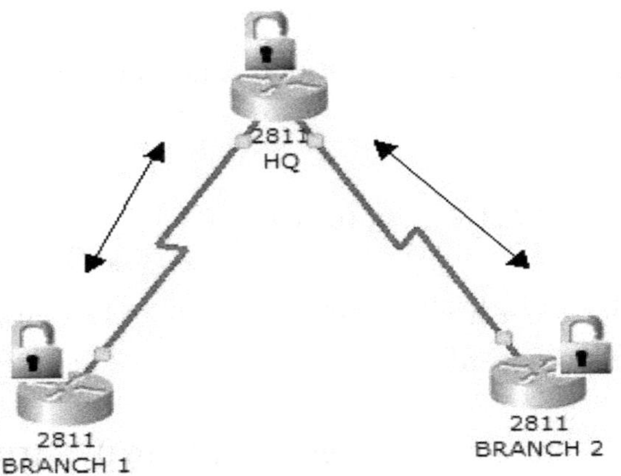

OSPF packets encrypted

To apply these settings must enter the console mode of the router "CPD2" and the serial interface 0/2/0 is the link directly connected to the house of the student and issue the following command:

Router (config) #int s0 / 2/0

Router (config-if) #ip OSPF message-digest-key 1 md5 7 a secret Router (config-router) #area 0 authentication message-digest

- Key [1] → is the number of processes.
- Md5 [1 - 7] -> The level of encryption
- [Asecret] → Is the password

Then activate authentication with the command area 0 authentication message-digest [Area 0] → is the area where we will introduce encryption.

NOTE: We must make this setting for each of the interconnecting nodes.

The Connection Between Different Areas

We can also configure the OSPF protocol in the different work areas and using a router backbone area. In our network, we could represent that configuration by placing the mesh in the area 0 and the frame relay connection by ospf in area 1.

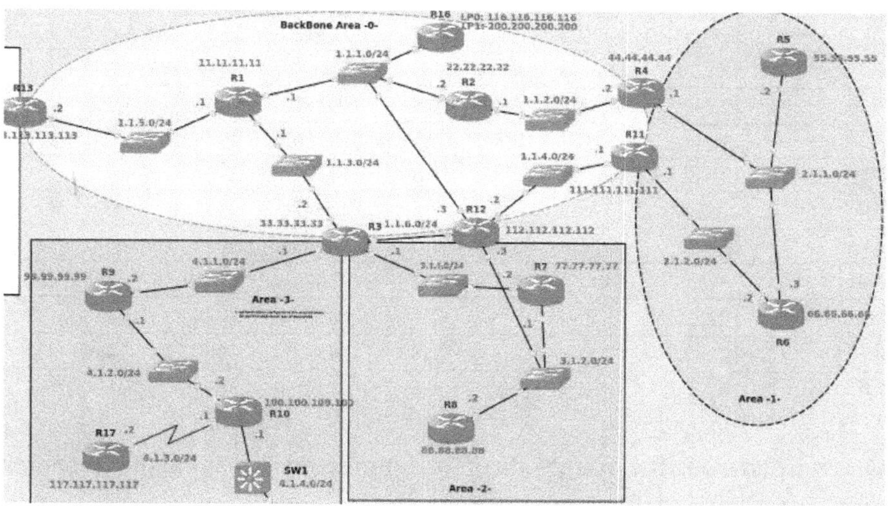

We apply this setting on the router backbone, in this case, is the CPD to connect the two areas all we have to do is create a new OSPF process containing the two areas as a rule.

Router (config) #router ospf 2

Router (config-router) #network 172.16.0.44 0.0.0.3 area 0

Router (config-router) #network 10.0.0.0 0.0.0.3 area 1

Router (config-router) #network 10.0.0.8 0.0.0.3 area 1

We will launch the show ip route command on some of the routers see how they mesh routing tables.

ID	O→D	Shortest path algorithm				Proposed algorithm			
		L	T	$\overline{C(t)}$	$\overline{Dest(t)}$	L	T	$\overline{C(t)}$	$\overline{Dest(t)}$
1	1→2	9220.4	1297.0	3.7	1.6	9611.9	1004.2	4.3	1.3
2	1→3	17334.4	6569.4	4.1	2.2	18265.8	2122.5	4.8	1.3
3	1→4	9612.1	2197.0	4.4	1.5	10039.2	1685.1	4.5	1.4
4	1→5	10180.7	1650.1	3.5	1.7	10632.3	1170.9	3.9	1.4
5	1→6	21784.1	4079.9	3.6	1.7	22773.8	2825.7	4.6	1.3
6	2→3	9542.3	1665.4	4.6	1.3	9717.7	1345.2	4.9	1.2
7	2→4	17997.7	3203.3	4.1	1.5	19291.8	2147.3	4.3	1.4
8	2→5	17845.3	2230.9	3.8	1.5	18266.7	1939.6	4.2	1.3
9	2→6	13545.9	2997.9	3.3	1.8	14225.6	2048.3	4.7	1.3
10	3→4	21473.6	3373.4	4.2	1.5	22042.3	2665.0	4.5	1.3
11	3→5	25722.3	8210.3	4.1	2.0	26920.6	3057.9	4.6	1.3
12	3→6	9377.0	1442.5	4.1	1.5	9450.3	1186.0	4.2	1.3
13	4→5	17222.2	2785.9	2.8	2.1	17980.5	2028.2	4.1	1.5
14	4→6	24187.3	4409.4	3.3	1.8	26523.4	3380.2	4.4	1.4
15	5→6	30704.2	4812.5	3.8	1.6	31428.6	3761.0	4.5	1.3

As we can see, the routes directly connected "C" and other routes through the OSPF protocol "O" where we find day by that network and that the next-hop interface. If we list the router "CPD2," We can see that the list routing table not known OSPF routes as we have encrypted the data OSPF sends its neighbors appears.

Chapter Four

ACL (Access Control List) Cisco

The main objective of this chapter is to help network administrators in the router configuration process, with its modest scope, this work intends to serve as motivation for the reader to seek new knowledge in the field of information security. There was no pretension here to exhaust the subject, but to provide the reader with a condensed text, bringing together concepts fundamental to the understanding of related terms.

The content of this chapter aims to address the configuration of access control lists (ACL) on CISCO routers. Initially, we will make some considerations about the hardware and software of CISCO routers. Next, we will discuss the concepts of access control lists and their implementation in the router.

Security has many faces, and one of the most important is the ability to control the flow of packets in a network to protect our networks from failure, degradation of services, theft, or compromise of data resulting from an intentional action or an error caused by users.

But an effective safety solution should not only be based on technical resources, and safety policy should be developed to define the institution's safety guidelines. To this end, there are international standards with the best safety practices, which can help in the process of security policymaking.

Before proceeding with the reading of this article, analyze item 9 - Examples, even if now you do not understand everything, because, with the visualization of the ACL, the understanding of the concepts becomes faster.

The Three As (AAA)

Access control is how you can control who has access to the network servers and which services you can use once you have access to them.

- Authenticate - Authentication is the method of identifying users who can use network resources;
- Authorize - Authorization is the method of remote access control;
- Auditing - Auditing is the method of collecting information about access, resource utilization, failed access attempts, start and end times for certain transactions, number of packets sent per protocol, among others;

In this text, we will focus on AUTHORIZATION. To this end, we will address the access control features that can be implemented in

CISCO routers, although the concepts can be applied to other access control elements.

It should be kept in mind that an effective safety system should not only be based on rules in the routers; other elements should be used, such as:

- Firewall
- IDS tools
- honey pots
- host security
- preservation and analysis of logs
- security policy

Cisco's operating system (IOS - Internetwork Operational System) provides several features that can be used to raise the security level of a network. Among these features is the packet filter, which will be studied in the next topics.

Basic Hardware Components

CISCO produces various types of routers. Although these products have considerable differences in their processing power and in the number of interfaces they support, they use a basic set of hardware. Figure 1 shows a generic schematic that highlights the basic components of a CISCO router. Although the CPU or microprocessor, amount of RAM and ROM, amount, and types of I/O port may differ from product to product, each router has the components referenced in the below figure.

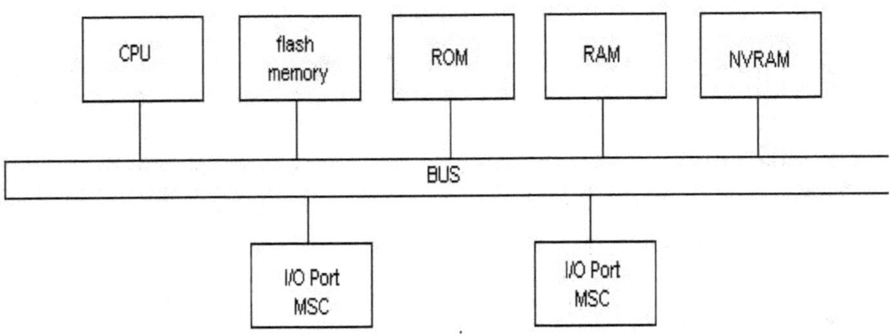

CPU

The CPU or mic-processor is responsible for executing the instructions that activate the router. The processing power of the CPU is directly related to the processing power of the router.

Flash Memory

Flash memory is a type of programmable ROM. This memory can be used to store various OS images and micro- router codes. This "dog" fun is useful for testing new images. Flash memory can also be used for trivial file transfer protocol (TFTP), an OS image to another router.

ROM

The ROM contains codes that perform startup diagnostics of the OST-like router (power-on self-test) performed by many PCs. In addition, a bootstrap program is used to load the OS.

RAM

RAM is used to store routing tables, buffer packets, provide an area to queue packets when they cannot be sent out due to the large volume of traffic routed to a common interface. In addition, provide storage space for ARP address information to reduce ARP traffic and improve transmission capacity to LANs connected to the router. When the router is turned off, all the information stored in the RAM is lost.

NVRAM

NVRAM (Nonvolatile RAM), unlike RAM, does not lose its contents when the router is turned off. NVRAM has a backup of the router configuration. This way, the router can return to operation without having to be re-configured. The use of NVRAM eliminates the need for an HDD or floppy drive in a router.

I/O and MSC (Media-Specific Converters) Ports

The in/out ports (I/O) represent the connections through which the packets enter and exit the router. Each input/output port (I/O) is connected to a media-spec converter (MSC), which provides the physical interface to a specific type of media such as an Ethernet LAN or token ring or RS-232 or V.35 WAN. Data is received over a LAN; layer two headers are removed, and packets are sent to the RAM. When these actions happen, the CPU examines the route tables to determine the exit port of the packets and the format in which they should be encapsulated.

This process is called process switching, in which each packet must be processed by the CPU, which queries the routing tables and determines where to send the packets. CISCO routers have another process called fast switching; in this form of the process, the router keeps a cache in memory with information about the destination of IP packets and the next interface.

The router builds this cache by saving the information previously obtained from the routing table. The first packet for a specific destination performs CPU processing to query the route tables. Once this information is obtained, it is inserted into the fast switching cache. This way, the routing tables are not consulted when a new packet is sent to the same destination. This way, the router can send the packets faster and consequently reduce the CPU processing load. It is worth mentioning that there are some variations as to the way of processing in some equipment.

There is another form of cache called NetFlow switching, where in addition to storing the destination IP, the source IP and TCP and UDP ports are stored. This feature is only available in larger capacity rotatores like the 7000 families.

The Process of Initializing the Router

When you turn on the router, some initialization routines are executed (See the next Figure):

POST - power-on self-test, during this process, the router performs diagnostics from the ROM; these diagnostics check the basic operations of the CPU, the memory, and the interfaces. After checking the hardware functions, the router starts the software.

IOS Image Location and Loading - After POST, the router searches the configuration log to determine where the IOS image is located. If the router does not find a valid system image or if the boot sequence is interrupted the system enters the monitor ROM mode; otherwise it looks in the NVRAM for the image location indicator that may be:

- *in ROM;*
- *on a TFTP server;*
- *in flesh memory;*
- *Once the IOS image is found and uploaded, it moves on to the next stage.*
- *Find and upload the configuration file - This file contains all the configuration information specified for the router in question. The configuration file is stored on the NVRAM, but you can configure the router to load it from a TFTP server. If it is not found a configuration file, the router enters setup mode.*
- *After the initialization process is completed, the router starts to operate. From this point, you can build new configuration parameters or change existing ones...*

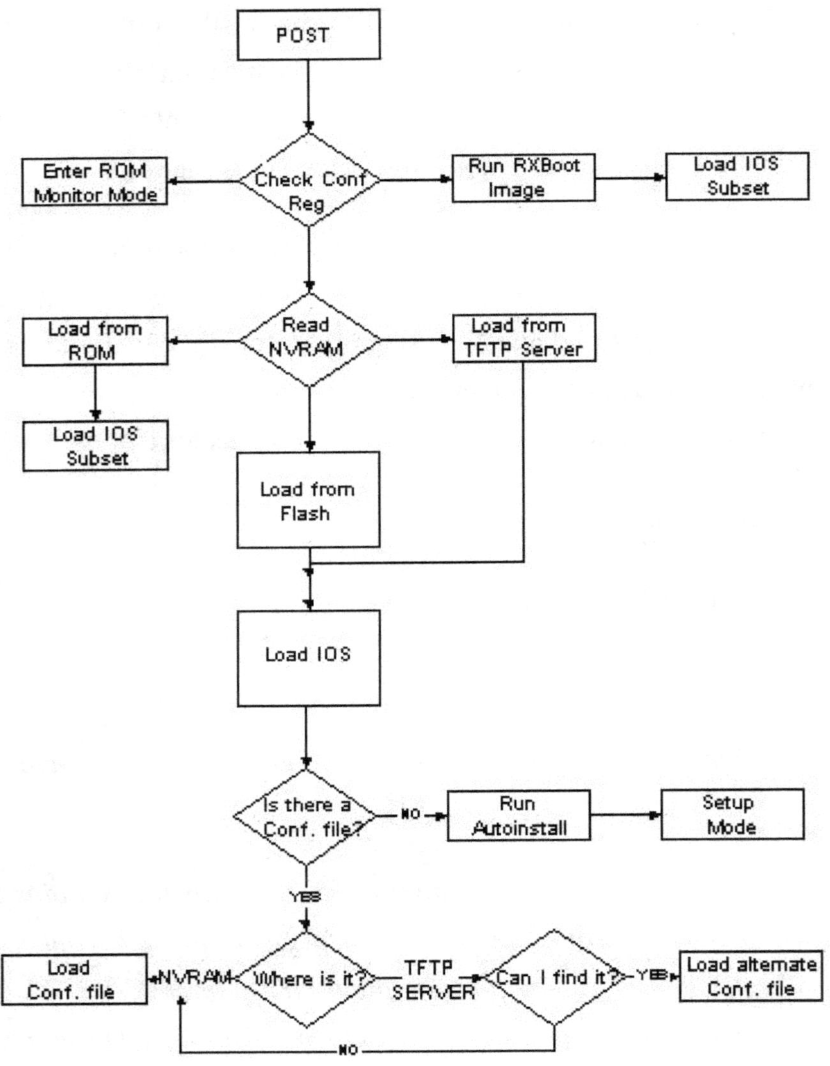

After booting, both the IOS image and the configuration file are stored in RAM, with the IOS image stored at the low addresses and the boot file at the high address, as illustrated in the next Figure.

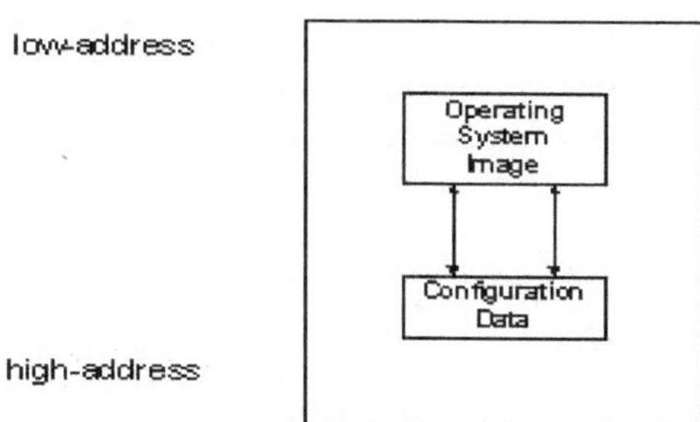

Data Flow

Once the router knows which interface type(s) it has (Ethernet, Token Ring, FDDI, X.25, Frame Relay, ...), it can check the format of the incoming frames and mount the outgoing frames, in addition, the router can check the integrity of the incoming data, since it knows the type of interface, it can calculate the cyclic redundancy check (CRC), in the same way, the router can calculate the CRC of the outgoing frames.

If the routing tables have only static routes, these tables will not be exchanged with other routers.

The ARP cache represents an area of memory where the relationships between the IP address and its physical address (the MAC address of layer 2) are stored.

Data that is received or prepared for transmission may enter priority queues, where low priority traffic is delayed in favor of processing high priority traffic. If your router model supports traffic prioritization, certain configuration parameters can be told to the router to indicate how to perform this prioritization.

Information about the data flow, such as the location and status of packages is stored in the hold queue.

The entries in the routing tables tell you the destination interface to which certain packets are to be routed. If the destination is a LAN and address resolution is required, the router searches the MAC address initially in the ARP cache. If the address is not found in the ARP hub, the router will mount an ARP packet to find the MAC address.

Once the destination address and encapsulation method are determined, packets are sent to the interface port. Depending on the volume of traffic again, the packet may enter a priority queue, hardware buffer, until it can be sent.

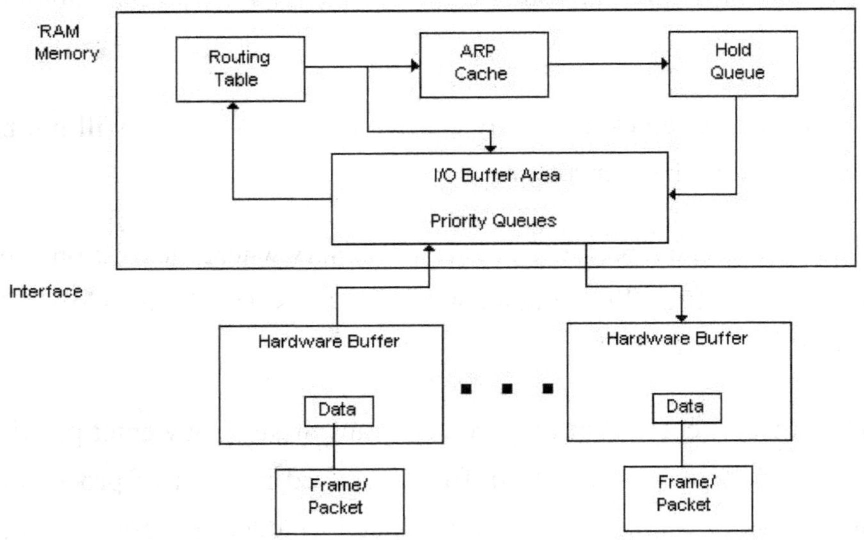

Traffic Control with ACL

An access control list (ACL) is a list of ordered rules that allow or block packet traffic based on certain information present in the packet. Let's look at this sentence in more detail:

- An access control list (ACL) is a list of ordered rules - this means that the order in which the rules are created in the access list is very important. One of the most common errors when creating access lists is configuring the rules in the wrong order.

- That allow or block packet traffic - first of all, it is important to know that at the end of the access list, there is an implicit rule that blocks everything. A package that is not explicitly will be blocked by the rule that blocks everything. Another common mistake when creating an access control list is forgetting this fact.

- Based on certain information present in the packages - this is usually information present in layer three or layer four package headers. Apart from a few exceptions, access control lists cannot use information from layers higher than 4 for filtering purposes. For example, an access control list cannot filter FTP commands. There's actually a way to do that... :)) using Context-Based Access Control (CBAC), which can filter packages based on known application information, but this subject will be dealt with in another article.

In addition to access control, the ACLs can be used for other functions such as:

- Dial on Demand - access control lists are used to define which packets are allowed for a dial connection (DDR - Dial- on-Demand Routing);

- Queuing Features - access lists can control what type of packets will be allocated in certain types of queues, for example, for priority control;

- Routing Update Filters - access lists can control the exchange of information between routers;

- Router Access - access list can control telnet or SNMP access to the router.

Note that these functions are different from packet flow control through the router.

Access lists can be configured for all types of routable protocols such as IP, AppleTalk, and others. In this text, our focus is TCP/IP.

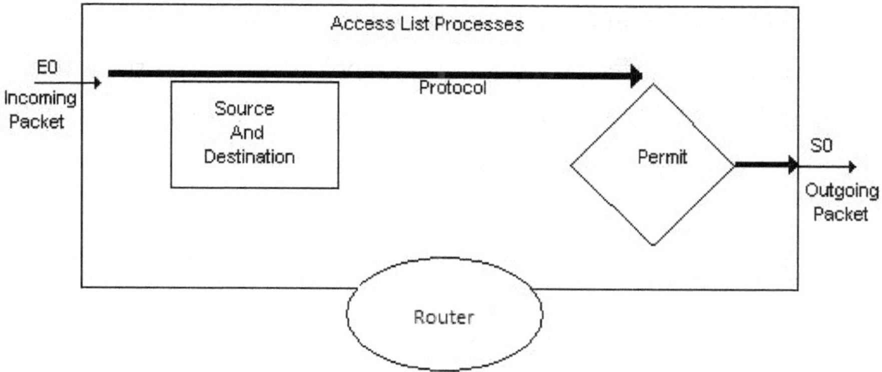

How the ACL Works

Package Flow-Through Access Lists

The process starts when an interface receives a packet. The router checks the routing table for a route to the package. If you do not have a route, this packet will be discarded, and an ICMP (unreachable destination) message will be sent to the origin. Otherwise, check if there is an access control list applied to the interface, and if not, the packet is sent to the outbound port buffer. Otherwise, the packet is analyzed by the access control list for the interface in question. Since the data flow through a given interface is bi-directional, an ACL can be applied in a specific direction of the interface:

- inbound - checks whether processing of the packet should continue after it has been received on a particular interface;
- outbound - checks whether the packet should be sent to an outbound interface or blocked.

It is worth noting that packets generated by the router as routing table switches are not affected by the rules applied to an interface in the outbound direction, the only way to control the packets generated by the router as table updates is through inbound ACL.

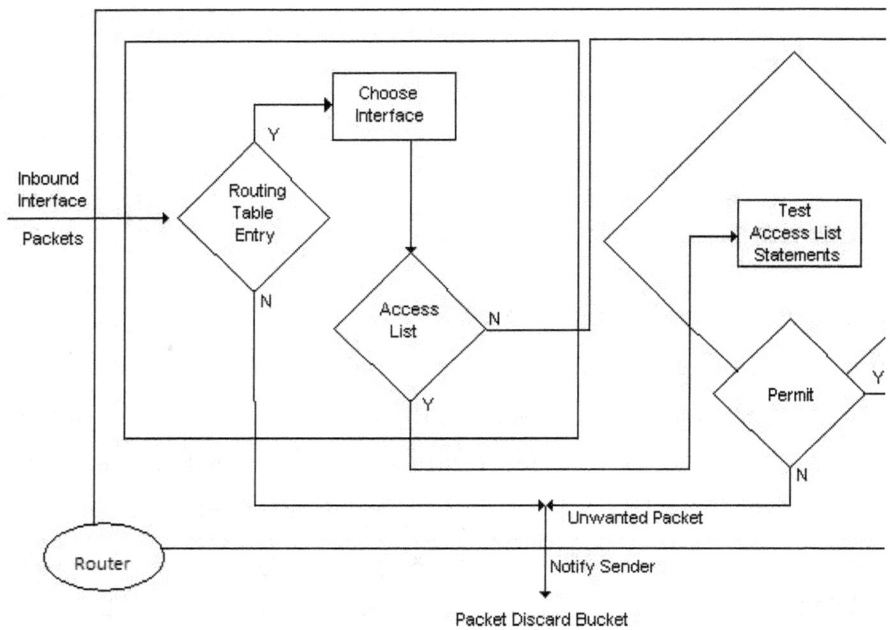

The access list is checked in sequential order; that is, the packet is tested from the first rule. Thus, if the packet fits into some rule and checking its condition - if allowed or blocked. If the packet does not fit any of the rules, it will be blocked by the last rule, which is implicit and blocks everything that is not explicitly allowed, as said before.

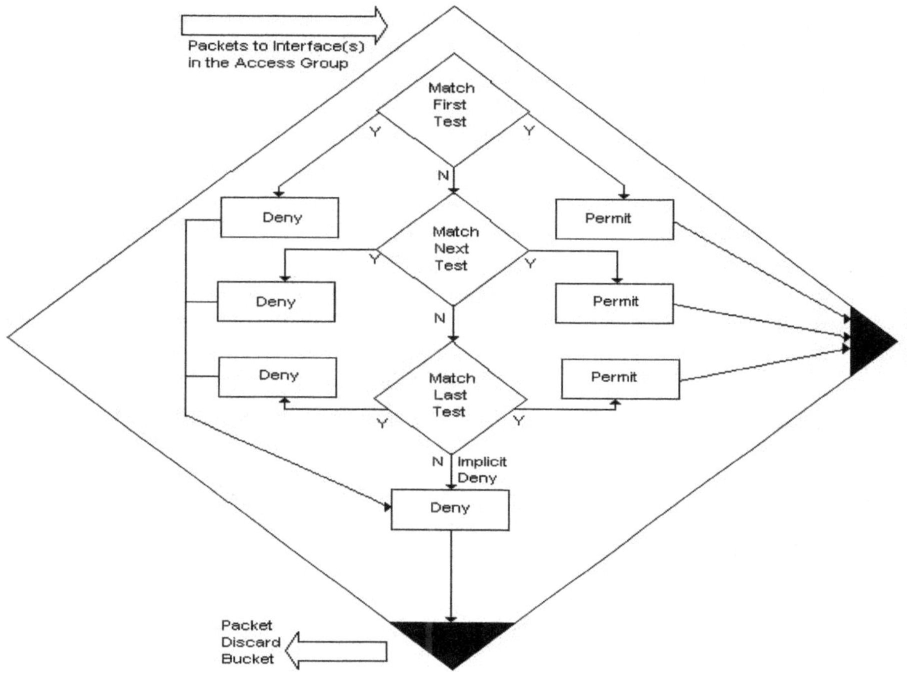

Types of Access Lists

The two main types of access lists are:

- **Standard** - The standard access list checks the source IP of a packet that can be routed. Based on the network/subnet/ host address, it is allowed or blocked to send the packet, i.e., that it will leave through another interface.

- **Extended** - The extended access list has more verification capabilities that can analyze source IP, destination IP, source port, protocols, and some other parameters, to allow the security administrator more flexibility in rulemaking.

Identifying Access Lists

When configuring access lists in a router, you must identify each unique list. In some protocols, the access lists must be identified by name. In others, they must be identified by number and some protocols allow identification by numeric number. When we use numbers to identify access lists, they must belong to a set of numbers that "identify" the protocol. Starting with IOS 11.2, it is allowed to identify the access list using names defined by the administrator, this for standard and/or extended access lists.

Based on the identifier, the router decides which access control software should be used.

Please see the tables below for the nomenclature grouping for access lists:

Access Type List	Number / Identifier
IP Standard Extended	1 - 99 100 - 199 por nome (IOS >= 11.2)
IPX Standard Extended Filtro SAP	800 - 899 900 - 999 por nome (IOS >= 11.2F)
AppleTalk	600 - 699

Protocol
Apollo Domain
IP
IPX
ISO CLNS
NetBIOS IPX
Source-router bridging Netbios

Protocol	Banner
IP	1 - 99
Extended IP	100 - 199
Ethernet type code	200 - 299
Ethernet address	700 - 799
Transparent bridging (protocol type)	200 - 299
Transparent bridging (vendor code)	700 - 799
Extended transparent bridging	1100 - 1199
DECnet and extended DECnet	300 - 399
XNS	400 - 499
Extended XNS	500 - 599
AppleTalk	600 - 699
Sourc-route bridging (protocol type)	200 - 299
Source-router bridging (vendor code)	700 - 799
IPX	800 - 899
Extended IPX	900 - 999
IPX SAP	1000 - 1099
Standard VINES	1 - 100
Extended Vines	101 - 200
Simple VINES	201 - 300

Implementing ACL

Finally, it is time for implementation. Initially, a topic that often causes confusion when dealing with access control lists will be addressed: wildcard masks.

Wildcard Operation in Cisco Routers

Address filtering occurs by using wildcard masks to identify what is allowed or blocked in the IP bits. Wildcard masks for IP address bits use number 1 and number 0 to identify what should be filtered into the bits of the IP.

- A mask ara with value 0 means that the bit must be checked;
- A mask with value 1 means that the bit should be ignored;

It is important to note that these bits are NOT related to IP Masks. The subnet mask is used to determine how many bits of an IP represent a portion of the subnet, i.e., the subnet determines which bits are important for defining a subnet. A binary set to 1 indicates that the IP address bit is part of a subnet, while a binary set to 0 indicates that the IP address bit is part of the host portion.

In the following example, we will see how bitmasks (0 | 1) block or allow packet traffic based on the IP address.

Condition test of an access control list with IP protocol: An administrator wants to test an IP address per subnet (172.30.16.0 to 172.30.31.0). The first two octets correspond to the network part. The third octet corresponds to the subnet (16 to 31); the fourth octet corresponds to the host.

The administrator wants to use the wildcard masks for IP bits to verify subnets 172.30.16.0 through 172.30.31.0. This is done as follows:

- Initially, the ara mask checks the first two octets 172.30, for this, it uses 0s in the wildcard bits;
- As there is no interest in filtering the host part the fourth octet will be ignored, for that the bits must be set to 1;
- In the third octet, where the subnet is located, the mask ara will check the position corresponding to the binary 16, that is, this bit must be with 0 as well as the upper bits, whereas the bits below the binary 16 must be ignored, for this to occur they must be set to 1s, so we have:

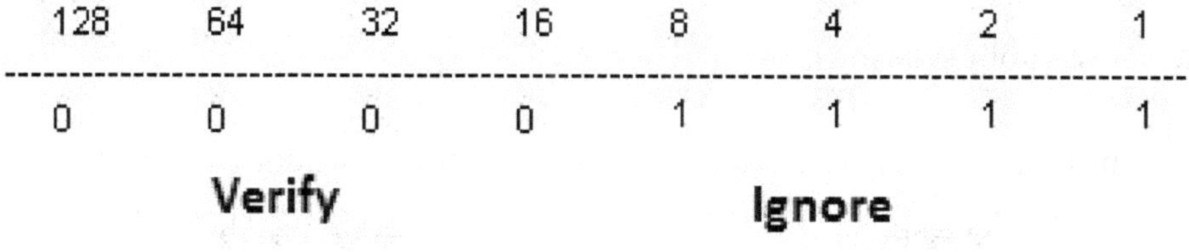

128	64	32	16	8	4	2	1
0	0	0	0	1	1	1	1
	Verify				Ignore		

O	**result**		**Final Is:**
For	o	Address:	172.30.16.0
With	a	mask:	0.0.15.255

The subnets will be checked: 172.30.16.0 to 172.30.31.0

Some abbreviations make it easier to use wildcards:

Let's consider a network where the administrator allows the entry of any IP address, that is, any destination to your network is allowed. To indicate any IP address the administrator should enter 0.0.0.0, now to indicate that the access control list should ignore the verification of any bit the mask ara should be set to 1s, ignoring the verification of any bit means accepting all, the final result will be:

IP Address: 0.0.0.0

Mask: 255.255.255.255

Result: allows/accepts any address

In this case, the mask for 255.255.255.255 can be replaced by **any** word (abbreviation).

Another possibility is when the administrator wants to create a rule that checks a specific IP address; given IP 172.30.1.29 the rule created is supposed to check the whole address, for this to occur all bits must be set to 0s, this way we'll have it:

IP address: 172.30.1.29

Mask: 0.0.0.0

Result: verification of the specific address.

In this case, the mask for 0.0.0.0 can be replaced by the word (abbreviation) host.

The use of incorrect masks can lead to the implementation of faulty access lists, as in the following example:

Let's assume that we want to allow all IP packets originating in the subnet 10.10.0.0 255.255.0.0 to host 160.10.2.100, and all other packets should be blocked. (If you don't understand the commands, they will be explained in the next content of this chapter).

absolute (config) # access-list 101 permit ip 10.10.0.0 0.0.0.0 160.10.2.100 0.0.0.0

absolute (config) # exit

absolute (config) # show access-list 101

Extended IP access-list 101

allow ip host 10.10.0.0 host 160.10.2.100

It may be noted that an access list was created using the mask 0.0.0.0. When we use the "show access-list" command, the router displays an entry with a "host." This means that the source address must be exactly 10.10.0.0, i.e., only packets with source IP address 10.10.0.0 and destination 160.10.2.100 will be allowed. All other addresses will be blocked, including 10.10.1.1, 10.10.1.2, etc. That is not what we want. Our goal is to allow traffic from all hosts on the 10.10.0.0/16 subnet.

You can notice that an access list has been created using the mask for 0.0.0.0. When using the "show access-list" command, the router displays an entry with "host." This means that the source address must be exactly 10.10.0.0, i.e., only packet traffic with a source IP address 10.10.0.0 and destination 160.10.2.100 will be allowed. All other addresses will be blocked, including 10.10.1.1, 10.10.1.2, etc. This is not what we want. Our goal is to allow traffic from all hosts on the 10.10 0.0/16 subnet.

Based on the example above, you should create a mask to check the first two octets "10.10" and ignore the last two "0.0". Remember that binary 0 means check and binary one means to ignore, based on this information, we will create the access control list again:

absolute (config) # access-list 101 allows ip 10.10.0.0 0.0.255.255 160.10.2.100 0.0.0.0

absolute(config)#	exit
absolute(config)# show access-list	101
Extended IP access list	101
permit ip 10.10.0.0 0.0.255.255 host	160.10.2.100

Now the command "show access-list" shows the new mask ara, this time correctly. The last two octets contain all the bits set to 1 (which is equivalent to the decimal 255).

There is, however, a more practical way to determine the mask to be used, I didn't say that at the beginning because I always use the military logic ", you can complicate air... to simplify air".

....:).

All you have to do is to subtract the subnet mask in decimal format of 255, this for each of the octets, let's see an example:

network mask: 255.255.224.0

wildcard mask: ???. ???. ???. ??? first octet = 255 - network mask = 255 - 255 = 0 second octet = 255 - network mask = 255 - 255 = 0

third octet = 255 - network mask = 255 - 224 = 31

fourth octet = 255 - network master = 255 - 0 = 255

wildcard mask: 0.0.31.255

This is the quick and easy way to determine wildcard masks. But the important thing is to understand why it works and not just lie about how it works.

Creating Access Lists

As said earlier in this section, we deal with standard and extended lists, so let's move on to the syntax of this type of list.

Standard

Remember that for standard access control lists, the number range used starts at one and goes up to 99. From the model shown in figure 15, we will assemble some examples of access control lists:

Example 1: Allow only packets originating in network 172.16.0.0: access-list 1 allows 172.16.0.0 0.255

Example 2: Block a specific host from the network 172.16.0.0: access-list 1 deny 172.16.1.30 255.255.255

Example 3: blocking a certain subnet: access-list 1 deny 172.16.1.0 0.0.255

Extended

For extended access control lists, the number range used for reference starts at 100 and goes up to 199. The protocols that can be filtered in the case of TCP/IP are:

- IP
- TCP;
- UDP;
- ICMP;
- GRE;
- IGRP;

For the access control lists extended the range of the operators are:

- lt (less than) - less than
- gt (greater than) - greater than
- eq (equal) – equal
- neq (not equal) - not equal

Example 1: Lock FTP for ETH0 interface:

access-list 101 deny tcp 172.16.1.0 0.0.255 192.168.0.0 0.0.255.255 eq 21

access-list 101 deny tcp 172.16.1.0 0.0.255 192.168.0.0 0.0.255.255 eq 20

Example 2: blocking telnet attempts out of the 192.168.1.0 network and allowing other traffic:

access-list 101 deny TCP 192.168.1.0 0.255 any eq 23

access-list 101 allow ip any

Implementing the Configuration Mode Access Lists

To implement an access control list, we must:

Enter configuration mode:

absolute# configure

absolute(config)#

Remove the current access control list:

absolute(config)# in the access-list number

Apply the list with the new rules:

absolute (config) # access-list absolute list number (config) # access-list absolute list number (config) # access-list list number

Select an interface to apply the access control list:

absolute (config) # ethernet interface 0

Apply the access control list according to the sense of verification:

absolute (config) # ip access-group list number {in | out}

To exit setup mode type: exit or end or CTRL-Z.

Write new configuration to NVRAM: the absolute (config) # write mem

Performance

Usually, performance and router are one of the main concerns of network administrators when it comes to implementing access control lists in routers. We know that access control list rules are analyzed sequentially, i.e., rule-1, rule-2, rule-3, and so on until a rule is found that matches the analyzed packet or finds the last rule that blocks everything that is not allowed. This way, we should observe some procedures that should be adopted to minimize the impact that accesses control lists can cause:

- Measure the router resources (memory, processor, others);
- Evaluate the services enabled in the router (encryption, others);
- Understand network traffic;
- Measure the volume of packets;
- Classify traffic volume by server, protocol, and traffic direction;
- The analysis of this information is of vital importance for the implementation of the rules to minimize possible impacts that may occur on the router.

A suggested strategy for implementation with attention to impact is:

- Whenever possible, apply the access control lists in the inbound direction, since in this way packets will be discarded before being routed to one of the outbound interfaces, thus minimizing packet routing processing;
- Initially, print the rules that cover the largest volume of transactions in your network, grouped by server/services;

- As the IP stack includes ICMP, TCP, and UDP. Always insert the most specific rules first, and then place the more generic ones;
- After implementing the list by server/service group insert a rule that blocks all other packets in the group, this prevents the packet from passing through the sieve of other groups to which it does not belong;

Keeping Configuration Files Backup

Backup maintenance of the configuration and IOS files is of fundamental importance, because eventually due to power failures, these files can be damaged or deleted from flash memory. In addition, the backup maintenance of the files facilitates the administration of networks with several routers. The network administrator has several possibilities of making backups; one of them is TFTP.

Ideally, there should be a dedicated segregated network for the network management function, which includes security management, this network should be isolated from the data network and provide out-of-band communication channels, in case of need to use data channels for management functions it is recommended to use secure channels.

Anyway, as the TFTP service does not require authentication, it is highly recommended to implement some mechanism that controls the origin of the connections to the TFTP server.

TFTP commands to backup and update files are:

- copy tftp running-config - Configures the router directly by copying files from the TFTP server to the router's DRAM.
- copy startup-config tftp - Backs up the NVRAM startup files to the TFTP server.
- copy tftp startup-config - Updates the boot file, copying from the TFTP server, and writing to the NVRAM.

See some examples below:

To load a new version of the IOS image to the router's flash memory, use the copy tftp flash command, as shown below:

absolute# copy tftp flash

System flash directory: File Length Name / Status

1 4171336 c 4500- j-mz_112-15a.bin

[4171400 bytes used, 22904 available, 4194304 total] Address or name of remote host [10.1.10.40]? 10.1.10.40 Source file name? c 4500-j-mz_112-15a.bin Destination filename [c 4500-j-mz_112-15a.bin]? Yes, Accessing file 'c 4500-j-mz_112-15a.bin' on 10.1.10.40 ... Loading c 4500- j-mz_112-15a.bin from 10.1.1.12 (via TokenRing1): [OK]

Erase flash device before writing? [confirm] yes, Flash contains files. Are you sure you want to erase? [confirm] yes

Copy 'c 4500- j-mz_112-15a.bin' from server as 'yes' into Flash WITH erase? [yes / no] yes

Erasing device ... eeeeeeeeeeeeeee ... erased Loading c 4500- j- mz_112-15a.bin from 10.1.1.12 (via TokenRing1):!

!!
!!!!!!!!!!!!!!!!!!!!!!!!!!!!!!!!!!!

!!
!!!!!!!!!!!!!!!!!!!!!!!!!!!!!!!!!!!

!!
!!!!!!!!!!!!!!!!!!!!!!!!!!!!!!!!!!!

!!
!!!!!!!!!!!!!!!!!!!!!!!!!!!!!!!!!!!

!!
!!!!!!!!!!!!!!!!!!!!!!!!!!!!!!!!!!!

!!
!!!!!!!!!!!!!!!!!!!!!!!!!!!!!!!!!!!

!!
!!!!!!!!!!!!!!!!!!!!!!!!!!!!!!!!!!!

!!
!!!!!!!!!!!!!!!!!!!!!!!!!!!!!!!!!!!

!!
!!!!!!!!!!!!!!!!!!!!!!!!!!!!!!!!!!!

!!
!!!!!!!!!!!!!!!!!!!!!!!!!!!!!!!!!!!

!!
!!!!!!!!!!!!!!!!!!!!!!!!!!!!!!!!!!!

!!
!!!!!!!!!!!!!!!!!!!!!!!!!!!!!!!!!!!

!!
!!!!!!!!!!!!!!!!!!!!!!!!!!!!!!!!!!! [OK - 4171336/4194304 bytes]

verifying checksum ... OK (0x29D5)

Flash copy took 00:00:30 [hh: mm: ss]

absolute #

To back up the configuration file, use the copy running-config tftp command, as shown below:

absolute # copy running- config tftp

Remote host []? 10.1.10.40

Name of configuration file to write [router-confg]? config_router_principal_2000-05-20.bak

Write file config_router_principal_2000-05-20.bak on host 10.1.10.40? [confirm] yes

Building configuration ...

Write config_router_principal_2000-05-20.bak !!!!!! [OK] absolute #

Examples

The purpose of this section is to demonstrate the process of rule creation. There is no intention to demonstrate a complete set of rules, and each network has its own characteristics, and filters must be created in accordance with the reality of the network.

If you do not understand what you are doing, you may have problems due to poor implementation of filters, so simply avoid copying the rules you find in the books and articles, but understand them before implementation. Anyway, check the articles listed in the link section, because they have an interesting set of rules.

Let's use the SMTP connection as an example of assembling rules to allow sending and receiving emails.

rule	direction	ip_orig.	ip_dest.	protocol	port_dest.	action
A	in	external	internal	TCP	25	permite
B	out	internal	external	TCP	>1023	permite
C	out	internal	external	TCP	25	permite
D	in	external	internal	TCP	>1023	permite
E	both	any	any	any	any	blocks

- Rules A and B allow email input
- Rules C and D allow email output
- The E rule is the default rule that blocked everything

Let's consider some examples of packages to make the rules easier to understand. Our SMTP server has IP 10.0.0.1, and someone on an external network with IP 172.16.2.3 tries to send an email to us. The source port used by the external client is 1234 with destination for 25, we analyze this situation according to the implemented rules we have the following:

packet	direction	ip_orig.	ip_dest.	protocol	port_dest.	action
1	in	172.16.2.3	10.0.0.1	TCP	25	permite (A)
2	out	10.0.0.1	172.16.2.3	TCP	>1023	permite (B)

In this case, the rules of our router allow the exit of the email packages:

- Rule C allows the client 10.0.0.4 to send the email to the server 172.16.2.1.
- Rule D allows the server 172.16.2.1 to reply to the client 10.0.0.4.

Now let's suppose that some located on an external network, 172.16.2.3, using port 4321 try to open a connection on the server 10.0.0.1 on the x-windows port 6000:

packet	direction	ip_orig.	ip_dest.	protocol	port_dest.	action
5	in	172.16.2.3	10.0.0.1	TCP	6000	permite (D)
6	out	10.0.0.1	172.16.2.3	TCP	4321	Permite (B)

In this case, the rules of our router behave as follows:

- Rules A and B allow SMTP packet entry.
- Rules C and D allow SMTP packet output.
- Rules B and D allow any connection using ports >1023.

Surely that's not what we want. To get around this situation, we must add one more element to our rules, the source port. Let's see how it looks:

rule	direction	ip_orig.	ip_dest.	protocol	port_orig.	port_dest.	action
A	in	external	internal	TCP	>1023	25	permite
B	out	internal	external	TCP	25	>1023	permite

C	out	internal	external	TCP	>1023	25	permite
D	in	external	internal	TCP	25	>1023	permite
E	both	any	any	any	any	any	blocks

Now let's look at the behavior of the rules with this new element:

packet	direction	ip_orig.	ip_dest.	protocol	port_origem	port_dest.	action
1	in	172.16.2.3	10.0.0.1	TCP	1234	25	permite (A)
2	out	10.0.0.1	172.16.2.3	TCP	25	1234	permite (B)
3	out	10.0.0.4	172.16.2.1	TCP	1245	25	permite (C)
4	in	172.16.2.1	10.0.0.4	TCP	25	1245	permite (D)
5	in	172.16.2.3	10.0.0.1	TCP	4321	6000	bloqueia (E)
6	out	10.0.0.1	172.16.2.3	TCP	6000	4321	bloqueia (E)

As we can see, after the inclusion of this new filtering element, it was possible to block the attack on the x-windows port.

But what prevents someone from trying to open a connection on the x- windows port, 6000, using port 25 as the source?

Let's analyze what happens in this situation:

packet	direction	ip_orig.	ip_dest.	protocol	port_orig.	port_dest.	action
7	in	172.16.1.2	10.0.0.1	TCP	25	6000	permite (D)
8	out	10.0.0.1	172.16.1.2	TCP	6000	25	permite (C)

As we can see, this package will be allowed, and the connection attempt will be successful.

To solve this problem we have to include one more element in our filters, this time we will include the analysis of the TCP packet flags, specifically the ACK flag.

rule	direction	ip_orig.	ip_dest.	protocol	port_orig.	port_dest.	flag	action
A	in	external	internal	TCP	>1023	25	any	permite
B	out	internal	external	TCP	25	>1023	only ACK	permite
C	out	internal	external	TCP	>1023	25	any	permite
D	in	external	internal	TCP	25	>1023	only ACK	permite
E	both	any	any	any	any	any	any	blocks

As you know, in the process of establishing a TCP connection, the first packet always has the ACK flag set to 0. The other packets on the connection have the ACK flag set to 1.

Now let's analyze what happens with the inclusion of this new element in our filter:

packt e	direction	ip_orig.	ip_dest.	protocol	port_orig.	port_dest.	flag	action
7	in	172.16.1.2	10.0.0.1	TCP	25	6000	ACK = 0	Block (E)

As you can now notice, attempts to open a connection originating from external networks and destined for ports >1023 will be blocked.

It is worth remembering that it is recommended to log all attempts to violate the rules because this way, you will be able to "know" the attempts to violate your security policy.

In the case of CISCO routers, rules A and B are translated into a single rule, as it has holes to keep internal tables with connection status. This feature is available in routers from other manufacturers. This rule would be translated into the following:

access-list	101			permit
tcp any host	<address_IP_serv_SMTP>	eq	smtp	

Now I will present a series of real rules. Carefully analyze each to understand its application. But remember, these rules may not represent the needs of your network, as stated earlier, each network has its own reality.

Listing 101 - Entry Rules

Clear the list to allow access-list upgrade 101

Restrict package source addresses

! prohibits addresses equal to internal IP (spoofing)

! access-list 101 deny ip <Class_C_Internal> 0.0.0.255 any log

! prohibits router interface addresses (land attack)

! access-list 101 deny ip <IP_Address> 0.0.0.0 <IP_Address>

0.0.0.0 log

! access-list 101 deny ip <SIP_IPAddress> 0.0.0.0 <SIP_IP_Address>

0.0.0.0 log

! access-list 101 deny ip <Eth0_IP_Address> 0.0.0.0

<Eth0_IP_Address> 0.0.0.0 log

! prohibits private network addresses (RFC-1918)

! access-list 101 deny ip 10.0.0.0 0.255.255.255 any log

! access-list 101 deny ip 172.16.0.0 0.15.255.255 any log

! access-list 101 deny ip 192.168.0.0 0.0.255.255 any log

! prohibits loopback address

! access-list 101 deny ip 127.0.0.0 0.255.255.255 any log

! prohibits bradcasting (prevents ping amplifying)

! access-list 101 deny ip host 255.255.255.255 any log

Allows internally initiated connections (TCP ACK = 1)

! access-list 101 allow tcp any any established

Service Restrictions and Redirection

! forbid access to TFTP

! access-list

! forbid 101 deny udp access any

to any eq 69 log X- Windows

! access-list 101 deny tcp any any range 6000 6005 log

! access-list 101 deny udp any any range 6000 6005 log

! prohibits access to SNMP

! access-list 101 deny udp any eq snmp log

! access-list 101 deny udp any eq snmptrap log

! allows access to port 113 / tcp and 113 / udp (identd and auth), but logs

! these ports are used in winoob / winnuke attacks

! access-list 101 allow tcp any any eq 113 log

! access-list 101 allow udp any any eq 113 log

! HTTP to HTTP server only

! access-list 101 allow tcp any host <IP_Serv_WWWAddress> eq www

! access-list 101 allow udp any host <IP_Serv_WWWAddress> eq 80

! SMTP for mail server only

! access-list 101 allow tcp any host <IP_Serv_SMTPAddress> eq smtp

! POP3 for POP3 server only (if external allowed) access-list 101 allow tcp any host <IP_Serv_POP3Address> eq pop3

! DNS x- only for secondary access-list 101 allowed udp any host <IP_Serv_DNS1 Address> eq domain access-list 101 allowed udp any host <IP_Serv_DNS2 Address> eq domain access-list 101 allowed tcp

<IP_Serv_DNS1 Address> domain

access-list 101 permit tcp

<IP_Serv_DNS2 Address>

domain

access-list 101 permit

TCP

host

<IP_Secund_DNS2 Address>

host

<IP_Serv_DNS1 Address> eq

domain

access-list 101 allow TCP host <IP_Secund_DNS2Address> host

<IP_Serv_DNS2 Address> eq

domain

! allows TCP and UDP packets only for non-OS private ports access-list 101 allows TCP any gt 1023

access-list 101 allow udp any gt 1023

! forbid everything else, but log access-list 101 deny ip any any log

Listing 102 - Exit Rules

Clear the list to allow access-list upgrade 102

! allow only internal addresses access-list 102 permit ip <Internal_Class_Address> 0.0.0.255 any

! forbid anything else and log access-list 102 deny ip any any log

As stated at the beginning, the main objective of this text is to help network administrators in the router configuration process, with its modest scope, this work intends to serve as a motivation for the reader to seek new knowledge in the field of information security. It was not intended to exhaust the subject, but to provide the reader with a condensed text, bringing together concepts fundamental to understanding the related terms.

Thus, I tried to describe the internal decision-making process of a router to allow the reader a better understanding of the resources present in their networks. Moreover, it is worth noting that the simple implementation of access control lists in a router is not enough to guarantee the security of a network, it is another resource that should be used according to the security policy and together with the other elements that compose the network security perimeter.

A firewall is a technology that allows various approaches, where we can call a simple element with firewall packet filters to multilayer structures with demilitarized zones.

Before carrying out any implementation, make sure you understand how all the rules created work.

Chapter Five

Dynamics Host Configuration Protocol – DHCP

Protocol Dynamic Host Configuration (Dynamic Host Configuration Protocol - DHCP) is an extension of the BOOTP protocol that gives more flexibility to administer IP addresses. This protocol can be used to dynamically configure the essential parameters of TCP / IP hosts (workstations and servers) of a network. DHCP has two elements:

- A mechanism for allocating IP addresses and other TCP / IP parameters.
- A protocol to negotiate and convey specific information on the host.

The TCP / IP host configuration information requests TCP / IP called DHCP client and host that provides such information is called the DHCP server.

DHCP is described in RFC 2131 Dynamic Host Configuration Protocol of host-. Here is the DHCP operation.

IP Address Management with DHCP

DHCP uses the following three methods to assign IP addresses:

a) manual assignment

The network administrator manually sets the IP address of the DHCP client on the DHCP server. DHCP is used to give the DHCP client the value of this manually configured IP address.

b) automatic allocation

It not required to manually assign IP addresses. The DHCP server assigns to the DHCP client, on the first contact, a permanent IP address can not reuse any other DHCP client.

c) dynamic allocation

DHCP assigns an IP address to the DHCP client for a specified time. After this period expires, the IP address and DHCP client is revoked must return. If the client still needs an IP address to conduct their operations, you must reapply.

This protocol allows automatic reuse of an IP address. If a DHCP client no longer needs an IP address, as in the case of a computer off harmoniously, it releases your address and delivery to the DHCP server. This can reassign this address to another client who asks.

The dynamic allocation method is very useful for DHCP clients that need an IP address for a temporary connection to the network. For example, consider a situation in which 300 users have laptops connected to a network, and it addresses have been assigned class C. This type of address allows the network have up to 253 nodes (255-2 special addresses = 253).

Because computers that connect to a network using the TCP / IP requires a unique IP address have, then the computer 300 may not operate simultaneously. However, if only 200 physical connections to the network can find an address of class C by reusing IP addresses unused. Using DHCP in its method of dynamic allocation of IP addresses, IP addresses can be reused.

Furthermore, the dynamic allocation of IP addresses is a good method to assign IP addresses to computers that are to be connected first and in a network where IP addresses are scarce. If the old computers are removed, their IP addresses can be reused or reassigned immediately.

Regardless of which method is chosen, you can still set the IP parameters at once from a central server, rather than repeat the TCP / IP settings for each computer.

THE PROCESS DHCP IP Address Acquisition

Once a DHCP client has contacted a DHCP server, through various internal states, it negotiates the use and duration of your IP address. The form of acquisition of the IP address by the DHCP client is best explained in terms of a state transition diagram (also called finite state machine). The figure shows the state transition diagram explaining the interaction between the client and the DHCP server.

When the DHCP client is initialized, it starts in the initialization state INIT. The DHCP client does not know its IP parameters and thus sends a DHCPDISCOVER broadcast. DHCPDISCOVER message is encapsulated in a UDP packet. The number 67 stands with UDP destination port, the same used by the BOOTP server because the DHCP protocol is an extension of this protocol.

DHCPDISCOVER message uses IP broadcast address 255.255.255.255 value. If there is no DHCP server on the local network, the IP router must have a DHCP relay agent that supports the relay this request to the other subnets. The DHCP relay agent is described in RFC 1542 standard.

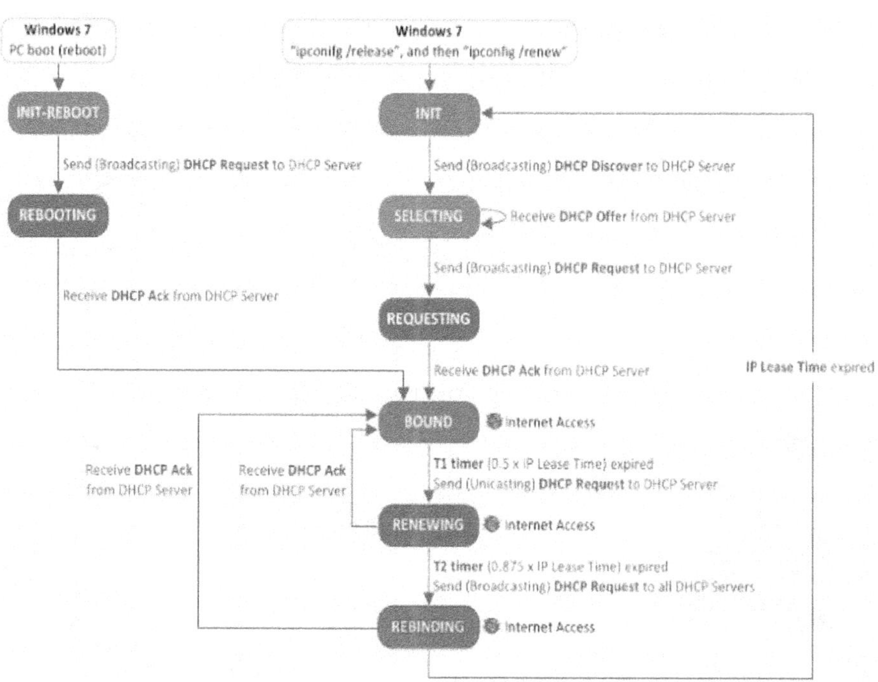

Before sending the message broadcast DHCPDISCOVER, the DHCP client waits for a random time between 1 to 10 seconds to avoid a collision with another DHCP client, as with all DHCP clients are initialized at the same time receiving all energy while (as a loss or interruption of electricity).

After sending the DHCPDISCOVER broadcast message, the DHCP client enters the SELECTING state where receive DHCPOFFER messages from DHCP servers configured to serve you.

The time the DHCP client will wait for the DHCPOFFER messages depends on the implementation. If the DHCP client receives several answers DHCPOFFER, will choose one. In reaction, the DHCP client will send a message DHCPREQUEST to choose a DHCP server, which will reply with DHCPACK.

As an option, the DHCP client controls the IP address in the DHCPACK sent to verify if it is or is not in use. In a broadcast network, the DHCP client sends an ARP request with the IP address suggested verifying that it is not duplicated. Should be, the DHCPACK from the server is ignored and sends a DHCPDECLINE, which DHCP client enters the INIT state and reorders a valid IP address that is not in use.

When the ARP request is broadcast on the network, the client uses its own hardware address in the source address field of the ARP hardware but places the value 0 in the source IP address field. This address value 0 is used instead of the IP address suggested, to avoid confusing ARP caches of other hosts.

When the DHCPACK is accepted from the DHCP server, three values of timing and DHCP client moves to the BOUND placed state (associated).

- T1 is the lease renewal timer.
- T2 is the reclose timer.
- T3 is the duration of the rental.

The DHCPACK always brings the value of T3. The values of T1 and T2 are configured on the DHCP server; otherwise, the values are used following default:

- T1 = 0.5 x T3.
- T2 = 0.875 x T3.

The current time when the timers expire is calculated by adding the value of the timer to the time when the DHCPREQUEST message, which generated the DHCPACK reply, was sent.

If this time is T0, then the expiration values are calculated as:

- T1 = T0 expiration of T1 +
- T2 = T0 expiration of T2 +
- T3 = T0 expiration of T3 +

RFC 2131 recommends that factor must be added to T1 and T2 to prevent multiple DHCP clients their timers expire at the same time.

After the expiration of the timer T1, the DHCP client moves to the BOUND state to the RENEWING state (renewal). In the latter state must negotiate a new rent for

IP address designated between the DHCP client and the DHCP server that originally assigned the IP address. If the DHCP server original, for some reason, does not renew the rent, will send a message DHCPNACK, and DHCP client moves to INIT state and attempt to obtain a new IP address.

Otherwise, if the original DHCP server sends a DHCPACK message, it will contain the length of the new rental. Then the DHCP client places the values of their timers and will move to the BOUND state.

If timer T2 (reclose time) expires while the DHCP client is waiting in the RENEWING state for a response from DHCPACK or DHCPNACK from the original DHCP server, the DHCP client will move to the REBINDING state. The original DHCP server may not have responded because it would be turned off or because the link to the network would have dropped. Note in the previous equations that T2 is greater than T1, so the DHCP client expects the original DHCP server to renew the rental for a time equal to T2 - T1

Upon expiration of timer T2 (reclosing time), the DHCP client will send a DHCPREQUEST to the network to contact any DHCP server to extend the rental, which will then go into the REBINDING state.

The DHCP client sends this DHCPREQUEST broadcast message because it assumes that, after waiting for T2 - T1 seconds in the

RENEWING state, the original DHCP server is not available, so it will try to contact another DHCP server to respond.

If a DHCP server responds with a DHCPACK, the DHCP client renews its rental (T3), sets the timers T1 and T2, and returns to the BOUND state. If there is no DHCP server available to renew rent after the expiration of the T3 timer, the rental ceases, and the DHCP client goes to the INIT state.

Note that the DHCP client tried to renew the rental first with the original server and then with any other server in the network. At the end of the rental (T3 expires), the DHCP client must return his IP address and cease all activities with the said IP address on the network.

The DHCP client does not always have to wait for the expiration of the rent to end the use of an IP address. This may give up voluntarily to an IP address, canceling your rental. For example, the user could connect a laptop computer to the network for a particular activity.

The DHCP server network address could place the rent for an hour. Assuming the user finishes their task in 30 minutes, then disconnected from the network at the end of that period. When the user releases harmoniously, the DHCP client will send a message to the DHCP server DHCPRELEASE to cancel the rent. The IP address will now be available.

If DHCP clients operate on computers that have a hard disk, the assigned IP address can be stored on this device and, when the computer restarts its operations, it can make a new request using this IP address.

Dhcp Package Format

The figure illustrates the format of the DHCP package, which is a fixed format for all fields, except for options that have a minimum of 312 octets.

op (1)	htype (1)	hlen (1)	hops (1)
xid (4)			
secs (2)		flags (2)	
ciaddr (4)			
yiaddr (4)			
siaddr (4)			
giaddr (4)			
chaddr (16)			
sname (64)			
file (128)			
options (312)			

Readers who know the BOOTP protocol recognize that the exception of the flag and option fields, the DHCP and BOOTP message formats are identical. In fact, the DHCP server can be configured to respond to BOOTP requests. The configuration details are specific to each operating system.

The following table explains the DHCP protocol fields. In the field of options, only the bit that is more to the left is used, as can be seen in the figure. The other bits of this field are set to 0.

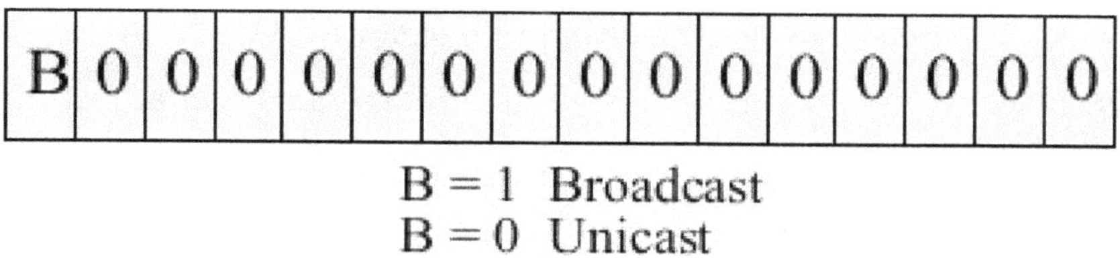

B = 1 Broadcast
B = 0 Unicast

Most DHCP messages sent by a DHCP server to their clients are unicast messages (that is, they are messages sent to a single IP address). This is because the DHCP server assimilates the hardware addresses of DHCP clients from the messages it receives from them.

A DHCP client could request that the DHCP server responds with a broadcast address by setting the leftmost bit equal to 1 in the options field. The DHCP client will do this if it does not yet know its IP address.

The IP protocol module in the DHCP client will reject any datagram if the IP destination address contained in it does not match the IP address of the DHCP client (network interface). If the IP address of the network interface is not known, the datagram will also be rejected.

However, the IP protocol module will accept any broadcast IP datagram. Therefore, to ensure that the IP protocol module accepts the response from the DHCP server when the IP address is not yet configured, the DHCP client will request that the response from the DHCP server use broadcast messages instead of unicast messages.

The options field is variable in length, with the extended minimum size to 312 bytes, so that the minimum size of a DHCP message is 576 bytes, so is the minimum size of IP datagrams that a host must accept. If the client needs to use DHCP messages larger size, it can negotiate this with the option of maximum message size DHCP (DHCP Maximum message size).

Because the sname and file fields are very large and not always used, DHCP options could be further expanded within these fields, specifying the option overload option. If present, the frequent meanings of the sname and file fields are ignored, and the options use these fields. The options will be expressed using the type, length, and value format (Type - Lenght - Value: T – L – V).

The following figure shows that the option consists of an octet for type (T), followed by a field octet of length (L). The value of the Length field contains the size of the value field (V).

1 Octate	**1 Octate**	**N- Octates**
Type	Longitude (N)	Value

The different DHCP messages themselves are expressed using a special type value equal to 53. The option values describing the DHCP messages are presented in the figure:

DHCP Message Type: Indicates the specific type of DHCP message:

Option Value	DHCP Message Type
1	*DHCPDISCOVER*
2	*DHCPOFFER*
3	*DHCPREQUEST*
4	*DHCPDECLINE*
5	*DHCPACK*
6	*DHCPNAK*
7	*DHCPRELEASE*
8	*DHCPINFORM*

Chapter Six

NAT - Network Address Translation

With the exponential growth of Internet usage, there is a possibility of scarce valid IP addresses, i.e., addresses that are routable on the Internet. In this context, it becomes a useful protocol that allows the growth of global network utilization not to be halted and that, at the same time, do not exhaust the addresses that are provided by IPV4 (Internet Protocol Version 4).

NAT, which is the protocol addressed in this paper, has been widely used by many network administrators to meet this demand.

The reason why NAT is so important is, as we said, that IPV4 provides a limited number of addresses (there are four octets, totaling 32 bits of addressing). With the advent of RFC 1918, rules were created that allowed the use of non-routable addresses on local networks, preventing any machine that wanted to connect to a network had to be recognized by a single and unique address all over the Internet. This creates isolated networks. There is still a need for these networks to communicate. That's where address translation comes in.

NAT typically operates on a router or firewall, which are devices that receive connections from different networks in their terminals, as we can see in the drawing below:

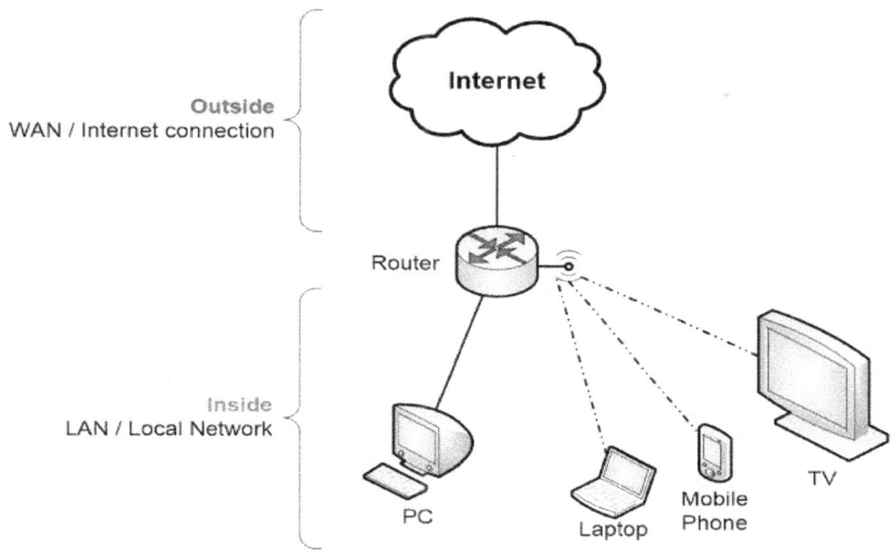

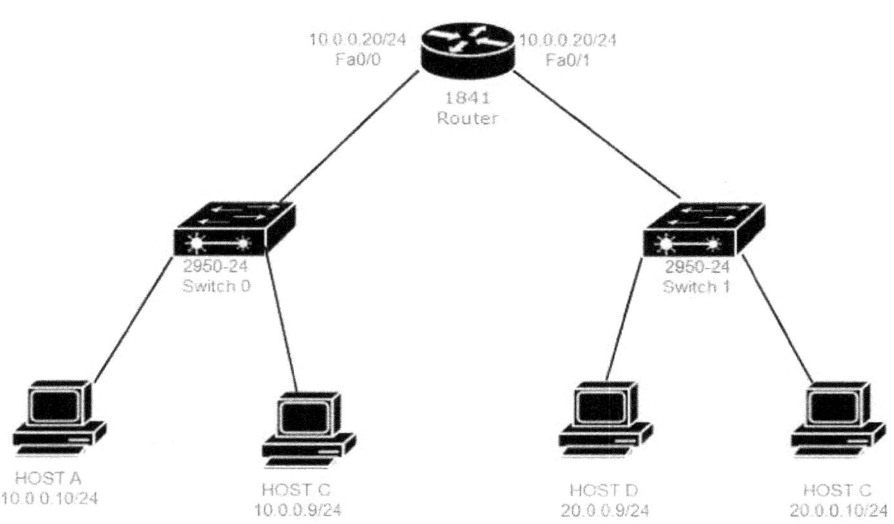

Note that in the two figures, there are 253 machines in the local network wanting to access the public or valid network. In a normal situation - without NAT - there would be a need for 255 valid addresses to provide this access.

With address translation, this problem no longer exists. You can assign non - routable addresses to the internal network and translate these addresses to one or more valid addresses.

Non-routable addresses are those defined by the Internet Assigned Numbers (IANA)

(Authority) for use on local area networks. According to RFC 1918, these addresses follow:

Addressing Class	**Address Range**
THE	10.0.0.0 - 10.255.255.255
B	172.16.0.0 - 172.31.255.255
Ã‡	192.168.0.0 - 192.168.255.255

Internet Service Providers (ISPs) benefit most from this solution by preventing them from registering a large number of addresses in IANA. In addition, companies can and manage your own IP addressing plan using and paying for a small number of valid IPs.

IP Connections - A Brief Review

Before detailing the operation of NAT, it is necessary to analyze the operation of a

IP connection. There are 65535 connection ports (the number of ports available is determined by the maximum value that can be generated from the 16 bits allocated to the IP packet port number). The first 1023 are reserved for the most common communication services known as WKS (Well Known Services), such as Telnet, FTP, gopher, www, and others. Because they are reserved, they cannot be used by other client processes.

Consider a connection between 2 computers, A and B. Computer A, by typing telnet serverB.com causes its operating system to select a port above port 1023 (say 1025) to open the Telnet section. Hence computer A connects B to port 23 - this is port reserved by IANA for telnet sections. However, the following information in the IP packet tells B that the source address of telnet opened the connection on port 1025.

This setting demystifies the idea that a connection between 2 machines is only made on one port - in the case of the example above, port 23. This item serves as the basis for the definition of Port Address Translation (PAT), to be discussed below.

Operation

Take, for example, a Local Users Wanting Server Access 200.244.37.76.

In this network, users of the local 10.40.1.0/24 network intend to access the search site server, which has a routable address (valid) 200.244.37.76. The administrator of this network followed RFC 1918.

But now you have a problem: how your 10.40.1.0 / 24 network - not routable - will access the where it is? The answer is obvious: NAT, for example, in the Firewall. As mentioned previously, this could be done on the router without problems.

With NAT enabled, the user calling the webpage in question in their browser will make your machine send a package addressed to 200.244.37.76. The source IP address (for example, 10.40.1.10) and the source port (for example, 1500) are in the packet, as is the address of 200.244.37.76) and the destination port (80). When the packet arrives at the Firewall, it will de-encapsulate it and rewrite it.

The packet it will send to the Public Network will contain the Firewall interface address connected to it - or another routable address previously set - as an address source port allocated from a list of free ports in Firewall, and the rest of the packet will be a copy of the original package.

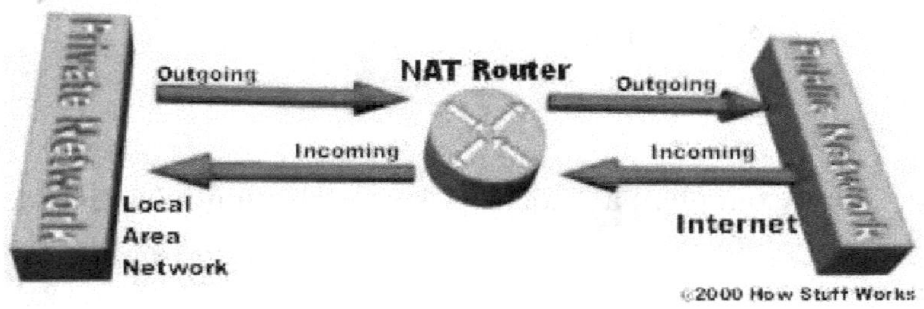

The firewall will also add an entry in a translation table where it will map the request for that is, and it relates the internal address that made the request and its port to the address and the port to be used as a translation. Below is a model of this table:

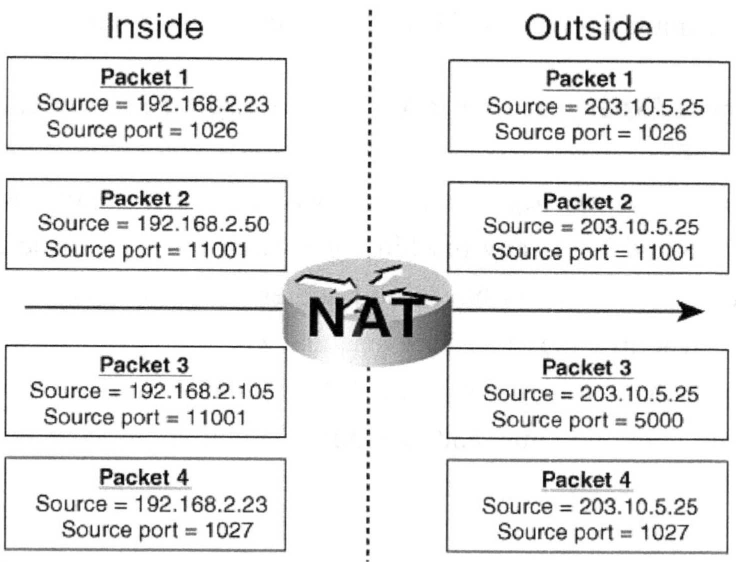

This information is vitally important for the next step of communication between machines. When the server responds to the request, it will respond to the firewall and not directly to the machine on the Internal Network. The packet, upon arrival in the Firewall, will be changed by it, respecting the translation table above. In the example, the packet arrives at the firewall with the destination address, for example, 200.182.30.1 and destination port equal to 45000. Firewall queries the table and verifies that it is equivalent to address 10.40.1.10 on port 1500, then making the necessary changes.

Transparent Bi-Directional Connectivity Between Networks with Different Addresses

This feature makes it transparent to network elements that are not directly involved with translating the use of NAT. For them, the IP packet that has been NATed is a packet like any other. Importantly, only the translator element "knows" that the address was changed.

Eliminate Expenses Associated with Changing Server/Network Addresses

As was said at the beginning of the work, without the existence of RFC1918 and NAT, any machine that wanted to be viewed on the Public Network should have valid addresses. In this situation, any change in addressing of a single machine would imply replicating the change in ALL routable machines. This would require a very high expense with the time and manpower required to configure the machines.

Imagine here an example where a network administrator resolves to change your ISP. In the situation above, to change your provider, the administrator should change the address of all machines on your network. With NAT, just make the change in a single point (translator element), and it will be responsible for providing the IP to the requesting machine - following RFC1918- the IP of the new range of IPs provided by the new provider.

NAT types

It is possible to practice three ways of address translation. Are they:

1. Static NAT

2. Dynamic NAT

3. PAT - Port Address Translation

Static NAT

As its name implies, static NAT defines a fixed machine translation address from Local to Public Network. This type of NAT is often used when you want to hide the internal addressing of a machine to the Public Network and also make it visible to it.

Dynamic NAT

This concept of translation, as opposed to the previous one, says that translation should only occur when there is a request that requires translation. In this technique, we work with a range of addresses that available to the translator device (Firewall or Router) to perform the conversion of Addresses. With each request made, it consults this range and uses the first free address that finds it.

This model is considered the most flexible as it allows several different solutions to do the conversion. There are three models of dynamic NAT:

- ***1x1 conversion:*** this NAT model is little used because it does not help in the control of the use of public addresses. He says that each requesting machine on the internal network will have a translation address on the public network. It only has the advantage of "hiding" the internal addressing.

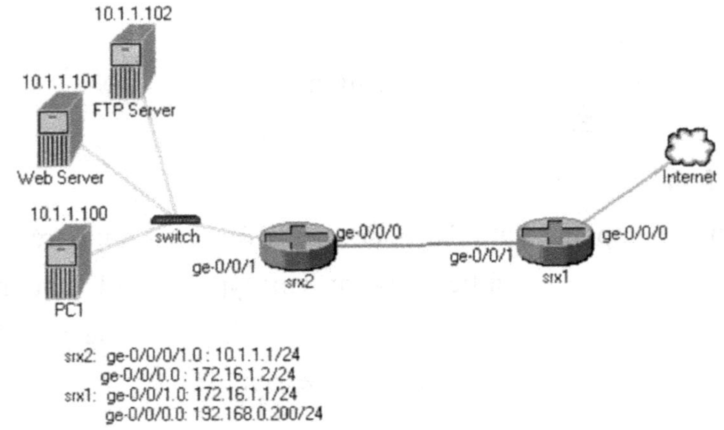

- ***N x M Conversion (N> M):*** This model is used when the amount of addresses on the internal network is greater than the number of addresses in the range. It is a mix between 1x1 conversion and PAT (to be defined below). The translator, upon receiving the requests, will use track addresses as if you were doing a 1x1 conversion. When the addresses, he starts doing Port Address Translation - PAT. This model is widely used when there is a need to interconnect two networks that are following RFC 1918. Following is an example of its use:

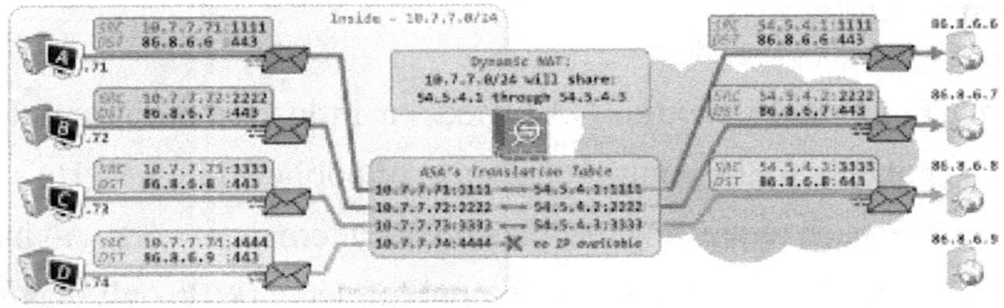

In this example, there are two local networks interconnected via a data link: one in location A (Matrix), and another one in place B (Branch). The headquarters machines intend to access the branch machines via NAT. In the figure above, it can be noted that there are fewer addresses in the NAT 192.168.1.0 with mask 255.255.255.0) than in the Local Network Headquarters (network 10.40.1.0 with mask 255.255.248.0). If all machines are going to make requests to the 192.xxx network when at the same time, the 10.40.1.254 machine will be the last to be able to associate your IP directly to a range address. The next machine, 10.40.2.1, will need to perform a Port Address Translation.

- Conversion Nx1 or PAT: this model, being widely used, will be better detailed in the next item.

- Port Address Translation: Port Address Translation - PAT - is the type of NAT that saves most valid addresses (routable) because the translation is done in the N to 1 model, i.e., all Local Network addresses are translated to a single valid address. This type of NAT is actually a special case of Dynamic NAT because, in this case, as in the previous one, the translations are done on-demand, i.e., the translation only exists when a request is made. This model has a limitation on the maximum number of simultaneous connections. How is it? As you know, there is a limitation on the number of communication ports - already mentioned earlier. There are a total of 65535 ports available for communication, and it is only theoretically possible to translate less than 65000 concurrent addresses (cannot count on service ports) WKS for translation). This limitation is not a disadvantage for the model because, except in cases of networks extremely large, 65000 simultaneous connections is a pretty acceptable number.

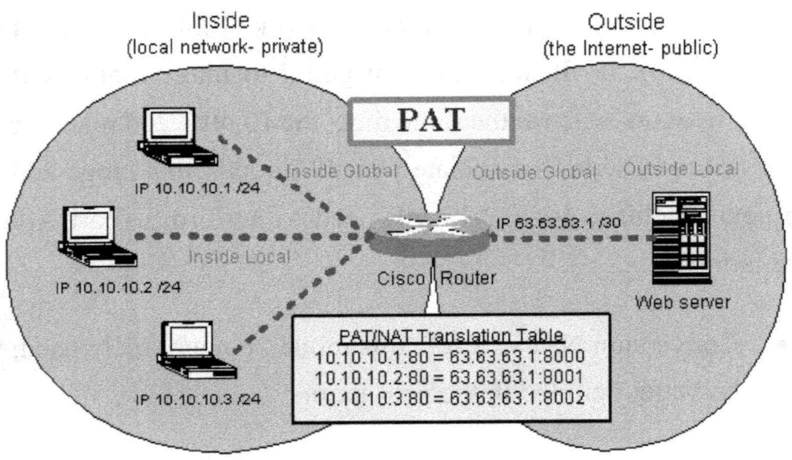

In the example, we have users allocated to network 10.40.1.0/24 - Internal Network - wanting to access the site A. Your network administrator has approximately 250 users in your network wanting to access the Internet, but the ISP (Internet Service Provider) only provided you with a range 200.182.30.0 / 29 which gives only three valid addresses. With this scarcity of addresses, the only solution to ensure simultaneous access to all is PAT. In this example, all leave with the address 200.182.30.1.

Below is an example of the translation device translation table (Router or Firewall), PAT based. It is considered the table with ten simultaneous connections.

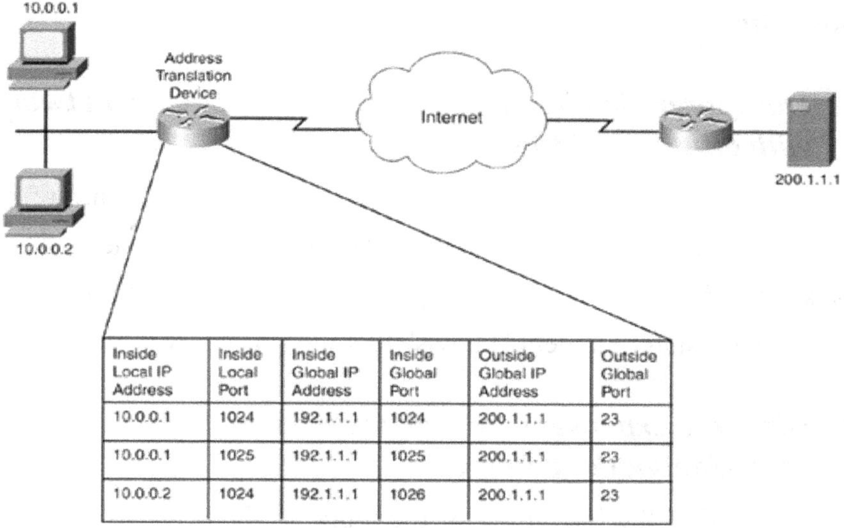

Inside Local IP Address	Inside Local Port	Inside Global IP Address	Inside Global Port	Outside Global IP Address	Outside Global Port
10.0.0.1	1024	192.1.1.1	1024	200.1.1.1	23
10.0.0.1	1025	192.1.1.1	1025	200.1.1.1	23
10.0.0.2	1024	192.1.1.1	1026	200.1.1.1	23

Note that all translations are done to a single address and that the ports cannot be repeated. Two special cases were marked in this table, one indicated with red color and another with the color blue. The first case shows that machine 10.40.1.2 is trying to open more than one connection to the Public Network (for example, it may be accessed - in the example - 3 addresses Web sites).

Also, note that the translator device (Firewall or Router) will handle this situation without giving importance to the fact that requests come from the same machine. For him, they are section requests independent. In the second case, there is a coincidence of 2 distinct machines opening connections using the same source port. Once again, the translator device will handle requests without the biggest problems because, despite having the same source port, have different source IPs.

Benefits

1. *Transparent bi-directional connectivity between networks with different addresses*

This feature makes it transparent to network elements that are not directly involved with translating the use of NAT. For them, the IP packet that has been NATed is a packet like any other. Importantly, only the translator element "knows" that the address was changed.

2. *Eliminate expenses associated with changing server/network addresses*

As was said at the beginning of the work, without the existence of RFC1918 and NAT, any machine that wanted to be viewed on the Public Network should have valid addresses. In this situation, any change in addressing of a single machine would imply replicating the change in ALL routable machines. This would require a very high expense with the time and manpower required to configure the machines.

Imagine here an example where a network administrator resolves to change your ISP. In the situation above, to change your provider, the administrator should change the address of all machines on your network. With NAT, just make the change in a single point (translator element), and it will be responsible for providing the IP to the requesting machine - following RFC1918- the IP of the new range of IPs provided by the new provider.

3. *IPV4 Routable Address Savings*

As stated above, there is better management of IP addressing with NAT. It is often said that there is now rational use of addresses. By reducing the range of addresses requested from the ISP, there is a reduction in the cost of links.

4. *Facilitates network design / implementation*

Due to the rational use of IPs, there is less concern with the creation of addressing maps facilitating their implementation/interconnection.

5. *Increases protection of local networks*

NAT avoids having to publish internal LAN addressing to public networks. Like this. It is more difficult for a malicious user to mount any kind of direct attack on the Internal Network. An attacker must attempt a direct attack on the NAT address before being able to attack the LAN. In addition to this advantage, it is possible to implement packet filters on the two elements that enable the Translation. In the next item, an example of using a Firewall as a translator and packet filter will be given.

Disadvantages

1. Unable to trace package path

Using translation makes it impossible to use the command traceroute <destination address> to identify the path that the package follows until it finds its destination because the translator element does not allow reverse translation (external to local network response) with a response indicating "timed out" - TTL (Time to Live).

The traceroute is a widely used command to verify connectivity between two points. If not If connectivity is achieved between 2 points, it is possible with this command to identify where the packet is "stopping" for lack of routes or interconnection issues.

2. Increased Translator Device Processing

As stated above, NAT requires the translation machine to change the IP packet. That maneuver requires the machine to devote part of its potential to this task to this task processing. For this reason, care must be taken in choosing the translator. Care should be taken to the extra processing demand. In this sense, equipment manufacturers use 2 product lines to perform the Translation.

They are:

- Software translation: there is an application that works on a server that plays the role of translator. The translation, in this case, is done via software.
- Hardware translation: in this case, the hardware is developed specifically to perform that function. The system is designed to optimize equipment performance when performing the translation.

The choice of the product line that will meet a certain demand depends on the need, i.e., the Right choice of product varies from case to case. Using hardware translation enables greater speed in translation and often lower deployment costs; however, there are limitations regarding the flexibility of the equipment.

With software translation, the opposite is true. The translation is done more slowly; the resources used are not optimized but allows great deal flexibility in daily use. Because it runs "on" an operating system, it is possible to use this last to incorporate new features into the application, for example.

Using NAT in Conjunction with Access Lists

As was initially said, there is a great concern with the protection of local networks. This concern is justified by the fact that these networks are often located servers that contain data of great importance (scientific research, customer data, etc.) and servers that are in production.

If malicious users hack these machines, and their data is corrupted, many interests will be seriously affected. NAT is known to have the advantage of hiding internal network addressing and that to gain access to a machine, and an external user will have to make a direct attack on two addresses - first the translation and

Then the real. However, simply using NAT does not guarantee network security. Attacks can be any of the 65535 ports on a computer. Here's an example where using NAT doesn't protect the network: Imagine that an internal network user A

Decide to access the Internet. It starts telnet on the public network. After a few minutes, he finishes the command and closes the communication window. Up to this point, everything seems to be pretty normal, but not easily understand is that the translating device will have, for a small but significant period of time, User A connection stored in their translation tables.

It is in this short time that a malicious user can take advantage and try to access the internal network. If it sends an IP packet on the port where user A would have the answer to his telnet connection, it will be accepted. This way, users from the public network may send IP packets to the internal network containing data that may damage any component on the network (bring down a server, etc.). It is in this context that packet filters act.

For convenience, the two elements mentioned in this paper as address translators (firewall and router) perform the role of a packet filter. They only allow them to pass packages that contain typical features that are described in the filter (for example, only connections on port 80 are accepted to server B or only accept connections from a specific public network address, etc.).

Here is a practical example. The presence of web servers is very common. This service, as has been said, is framed in WKS - port 80. So no other ports should be cleared for access, that is, any attempt to connect to a port other than this port may be considered as an attempt to invasion.

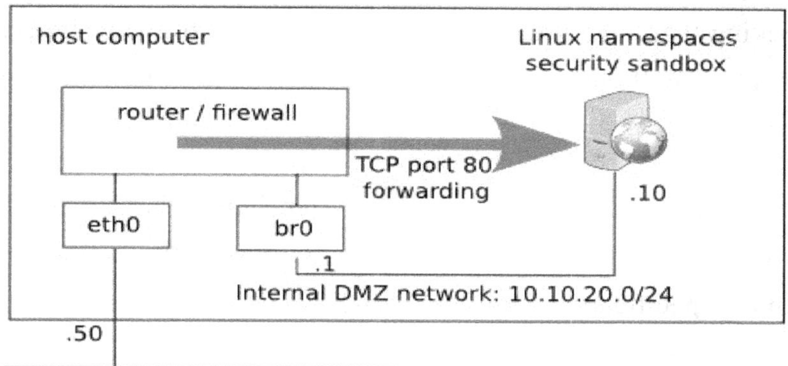

In the example above, a public IP user tries to access the webserver on port 80. To access lo, it first requests the virtual address (200.182.30.9). This one sends the information Firewall, and it will check if any rules allow packets to the web server on the port

80. In the example, the firewall will have this rule and allow the packet to pass through it. The rest of this process works like a normal NAT. In the next example, the same user will try to access port 1433 on the same server.

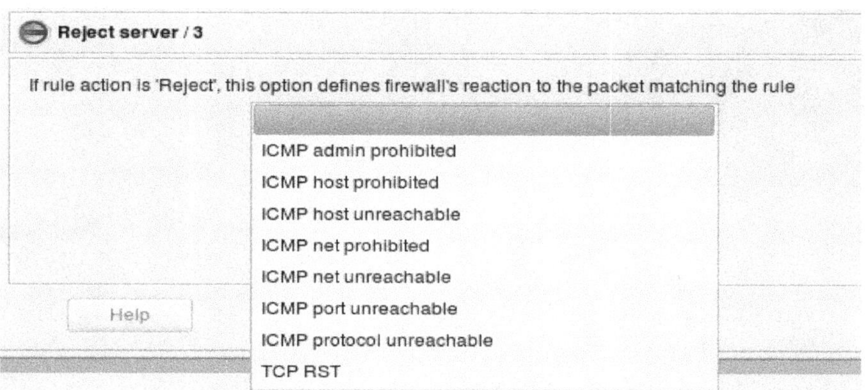

The operation is the same as shown above, and the Firewall, when checking that there are no rules allowing access to the webserver on port 1433, will discard the packet that arrived at it, not allowing the connection.

It can be concluded that using address translation - NAT - allows the use of IPV4 addressing more smartly and rationally, in conjunction with the specifications proposed in RFC1918.

In addition to the pure addressing issue, it allows you to increase the security of your local networks against possible attacks by external users to compromise the data structure that is maintained locally. This increased security is achieved by the fact that external users become unable to know local addressing.

For these and other reasons, it is believed that NAT will be increasingly used by administrators worldwide network.

Conclusion

Communication has always been one of the greatest needs of human society. As civilizations grew, occupying ever more geographically dispersed areas, long-distance communication became a growing need and a challenge. Ways of communicating through smoke signals or homing pigeons were the ways found by our ancestors to try to bring distant communities closer together.

Inventing the telegraph in 1838, Samuel F. B. Morse ushered in a new era in communications. In the first telegraphs used in the nineteenth century, messages were encoded in binary symbol strings (Morse code) and then transmitted manually by an operator through an electrical pulse generator. From then on, communication through electrical signals went through a major evolution, giving rise to most of the major communication systems found today, such as the telephone, radio and television.

This evolution in information processing did not happen only in the area of communication. Information processing and storage equipment have also been the subject of major investments throughout our development. The introduction of computer networks in the 1950s was probably the greatest advance of the century in this regard.

The union of these two technologies - communication and information processing - has revolutionized the world today, opening the frontiers with new forms of communication, and thus enabling greater effectiveness of computer systems. Such systems have undergone a major evolution from their inception in the postwar period to the present day.

Although the computer industry is young compared to industries such as automotive and air transportation, computers have made tremendous progress in a short time. During its first two decades of existence, computer systems were highly centralized; usually in a single large room, the computer is a large and complex machine operated by highly skilled people. The notion that within twenty years, equally powerful, considerably smaller computers, could be mass-produced was considered unfeasible.

However, in the 1970s, the introduction of PCs revolutionized these computing systems, replacing the single computer model serving all the computing needs of one organization with another in which a large number of separate but interconnected computers perform this task. Through this distribution of computational power came then the computer network architectures we find today.

The Internet is a compilation of interconnected networks, and the connecting points are the routers. These, in turn, are organized hierarchically, where some routers are only used to exchange data between groups of networks controlled by the same administrative authority, while other routers also communicate between administrative authorities. The entity that controls and manages a group of networks and routers is called an Autonomous System [RFC 1930].

As we already have learned that the router is a hardware device for computer network interconnection that operates in layer three (network level). A router is a device for the interconnection of computer networks that allows ensuring the routing of packets between networks or to determine the route that the data packet must take.

A router is a general-purpose device designed to segment the network, with the idea of limiting broadcast traffic and providing security, control, and redundancy between individual broadcast domains, it can also provide firewall service and economic access to a WAN. When operating on a layer greater than that of the switch, the router distinguishes between different network protocols, such as IP, IPX, AppleTalk, or DECnet. This allows you to make a smarter decision than the switch when forwarding the packets.

The router performs two basic functions:

- The router is responsible for creating and maintaining routing tables for each network protocol layer; these tables are created either statically or dynamically. In this way, the router extracts the destination address from the network layer and makes a sending decision based on the content of the protocol specification in the routing table.

- The intelligence of a router allows you to select the best route, based on various factors, rather than the destination MAC address. These factors may include the hop count, line speed, transmission cost, delay and traffic conditions. The disadvantage is that the additional process of processing frames by a router can increase the waiting time or reduce the performance of the router when compared to a simple switch architecture.

Routing is understood as the actions that a router takes to send packets from an origin to a final destination, passing through different types of networks, the routers operate with the IP address of the packets. Therefore they operate in layer 3 of the OSI model.

The router must, therefore, make decisions that allow it to send packets through network traffic efficiently, then perform an evaluation of the optimal route for the traffic to reach its destination. This is what is known as routing protocols, which are used to build routing tables. When the most optimal route is determined (depending on the type of routing), those "paths" used to send the information from one path to the other, once stored, are stored, depending on the routing criteria each time packets are to be sent It is done according to the standards established by the tables.

A switch or switch is a network interconnection device, which segments the network into small collision domains, designed to solve performance problems, due to small bandwidth — obtaining a greater bandwidth for each final station accelerating the packet output and reducing the waiting time. It operates on the data link layer of the OSI model (layer 2).

A switch is sometimes described as a multiport bridge, and this is because a typical bridge can have only two ports that link two network segments, and a switch can have several ports, depending on the number of network segments that need to be connected. The switches store certain information about the data packets that are received from the different computers in the network, to construct sending tables, and to be able to determine the destination of the data that is being sent from one computer to another in the network. Therefore the table contains the physical addresses (MAC) of the devices connected to their ports.

Ethernet switches are becoming solutions for widespread use connectivity because they improve network performance, speed and bandwidth, relieving congestion on Ethernet LANs, reducing traffic, and increasing bandwidth.

However, a single LAN is subject to certain limits, such as the number of stations that can be connected to it, the speed of data transmission between stations, or how much traffic the network can support. To overcome these limitations, the so-called internetworks emerged from the 1980s. Internetworking is the science of interconnecting individual LANs to create WANs and connecting WANs to create even larger WANs. A Local Area Network (LAN) is a computer network that spans a relatively small area, while a Wide Area

Network (WAN) is a network that occupies a larger geographical area, usually consisting of two or more LAN's. These interconnect calls are performed by specific devices, such as routers, which are the subject of the next item.

At the end of this book, we can conclude that the routing and switching are of great importance within a network topology, since this technology allows, in addition to managing and controlling access to information, the sharing of resources and services between geographically dispersed networks. As a consequence, it is essential that the network administrator has complete command over the resources of the routing and switching terminologies that manages it, as well as understanding the protocols and design, as it will be possible to guarantee a higher quality in its performance.

In addition, we can also observe how important it is to implement an appropriate security policy that guarantees the integration of information on two devices that are compiled, protecting these assimilations and machines from external attacks, which could cause serious damage to the structure administrative and technical of a company or organization.

References:

https://www.cisco.com/c/en/us/training-events/training-certifications/certifications/associate/ccna-routing-switching.html

https://learningnetwork.cisco.com/community/certifications/ccna

http://mirelucx.over-blog.com/

https://www.cisco.com/c/en/us/products/collateral/security/ group-encrypted-transport-vpn/deployment_guide_c07-624088.pdf

https://stason.org/TULARC/security/firewalls/ 26-Implementation-filtering-rules-for-a-Cisco.html

https://lists.sans.org/pipermail/list/2003-June/008836.html

https://networkengineering.stackexchange.com/a/39665

http://www.cisco.com/web/about/ac123/ac147/about_cisco_the_internet_protocol_journal.html

https://www.cisco.com/c/en_ca/training-events/career-certifications/associate/ccna-routing-switching.html

https://www.netacad.com/courses/networking/ccna-switching-routing-wireless-essentials

https://www.globalknowledge.com/us-en/training/certification-prep/brands/cisco/section/routing-and-switching/ccna-routing-and-switching/

https://networklessons.com/cisco/ccna-routing-switching-icnd1-100-105/how-to-study-for-cisco-ccna-rs